We Sing and Praise

MUSIC SERIES FOR CATHOLIC SCHOOLS

We Sing and Dance

BY

SISTER CECILIA, S.C., M.F.A.

Supervisor of Music, *Sisters of Charity of Seton Hill*
Greensburg, Pennsylvania

SISTER JOHN JOSEPH, C.S.J., Ph.D.

Director of Department of Music, *Fontbonne College*
St. Louis, Missouri

SISTER ROSE MARGARET, C.S.J., M.M.

Supervisor of Music in Elementary Schools
Sisters of Saint Joseph of Carondelet, St. Louis, Missouri

Illustrations by RUTH WOOD *and* BERYL BAILEY-JONES

Ginn and Company

Boston · New York · Chicago · Atlanta · Dallas · Palo Alto · Toronto

© COPYRIGHT, 1957, BY GINN AND COMPANY
PHILIPPINES COPYRIGHT, 1957, BY GINN AND COMPANY

No part of this book protected by the copyright hereon may be reproduced in any form without written permission of the publisher.

Acknowledgments

Acknowledgment is due to publishers, composers, and authors for permission to reprint songs and poems in this book, as follows:

Ave Maria, "A Little Pumpkin" (words only) by Anobel Armour, and "A Little Tree Went Shopping" (words only) by Grace Stone Field; *Children's Activities,* "The Baker" (words only) by Marguerite Gode, and "The Peanut Man" (words only) by May Pynchon; The John Day Company, "The First Snow" (words only) by Alice Wilkins from *The Golden Flute,* Hubbard and Babbitt; Nona Keen Duffy, "Good Morning" (words only); Ginn and Company, "Down the Stream," "The Cobbler" (words only), "Sunday and Monday," and "The Postman" (words only) from the *Music Education Series*; Ginn and Company and the editors of *The World of Music,* "The Baker" (melody only), "Beautiful Spring" (melody only), "Fairy Fiddles," "Froggie Jim and Froggie Jill" (words only), "Jolly Little Eskimo," "Loving Care," "Moon," "My Mother," "Pretty Girls and the Shoemaker," "Raise Our Flag," "Six Little Mice," "The Three Wise Men," "A Thousand Stars," "Wooden Shoes"; Ginn and Company and the editors of *Our Singing World,* "Father's Valentine," "Flowers for Sale," "Girls and Boys, Come Out to Play," "Oh, Who Is So Merry," "One, Two, Buckle My Shoe," "Sleepy Song," "Snow-white Little Burro"; *Little Mine,* Publications for Catholic Youth, "Easter Bells" (words only); Longmans, Green and Company, Ltd., "To the Child Jesus" by Rev. W. Roche from *Child's Prayers to Jesus*; The Macmillan Company, "High, Betty Martin" from *Folk Songs of Old New England* by Eloise Hubbard Linscott, copyright 1939; *Mine, Two,* Publications for Catholic Youth, "The Christ Child" (words only) and "Easter" (words only); Isla Richardson, "November" (words only) from *My Bed Time Game*; Frank Scully, owner of the copyright, "Hush-a-Bye, My Baby" (words only); Dr. Mary Synon, "Saint Martin" (words only); Mary Dixon Thayer, "My Fairy" (words only); Western Printing & Lithographing Company, "The Song of the Three Little Kittens" (words only).

The second stanza of the song "Beautiful Spring" is used by courtesy of Sister Francis Borgia, C.C.V.I.; the songs "O Little Star" and "Winter Winds" by courtesy of Sister Mary Grace, S.S.M.; the words of the songs "Morning Prayer," "Little Things," and "Gratitude" by courtesy of Sister M. Immaculata, S.S.J.; the words of the songs "A Christmas Wish," "God Made This Lovely Earth," and "Lullaby, Little Jesus" by courtesy of Sister M. Josita, O.S.F.; and the words of the song "Gay Autumn Leaves" by courtesy of Sister Mary Luke, O.S.U.

"God, Our Loving Father" is found in Davison and Surette's *140 Folk-Songs* (Concord Series No. 3), published by the E. C. Schirmer Music Company, owners of the copyright, and is used with their permission.

In the case of some poems for which acknowledgment is not given, we have earnestly endeavored to find the original source and to procure permission for their use, but without success.

The contents of this book have received the approval of the DIOCESAN MUSIC COMMISSION, Boston, Massachusetts.

J.M.J.
Seton Home Study School

Music Book

Families have indicated to us that they are primarily interested in the Catholic and patriotic songs from the book that we previously provided for the music course. They find that other song gooks may be obtained from their library if needed. We have, therefore, put together a selection of Catholic and patriotic songs chosen from the formerly used music book. Since this is a collection of selected songs from the original book the pagination of the two books will not coincide. You may follow the provided lesson plans by following the Liturgical Year Sections as listed in the Table of Contents.

Contents

After Pentecost

God, Our loving Father 9
When I Look at the Sky 10
Maiden Mother, Meek and Mild 10
Moon 11
The Stars 11
Gratitude 12
Sleepy Song 12
Raise Our Flag 13
Timothy's Flute 13
Indian Hunter 14
Are You Sleeping? 14
Lights 15
Telling Time 15
My Angel 16
Dear Angel Ever at My Side 16
St. Frnacis of Assisi 17
God's Darkness 17
Christ, King of Glory 18
Father, We Praise You 18
Saint Martin 19
Our Country's Banner 19
Little Bunnies 20
November 20
Father, We Thank Thee 21

Advent

Come, Lord Jesus 22
The Advent Wreath 22
Veni, Domine Jesu 23
O Come, Ocome, Emmanuel 23
Mary, Our Mother 24
Sunday and Monday 24

Christmastide and After

O Come, All Ye Faithful(Adeste Fideles) 25
Christ Was Born in Behtlehem 26
I Saw Three Ships 26
Our Lady Came to Bethlehem 27
Hasten, O Shepherds 28
Winds Throug' the Olive Trees 28
The Christ Child 29
A Christmas Wish 29
Silent Night 30

Oh, Come Little Children 31
The First Christmas 32
    When Christ Came to Earth 33
    The Father Was Watching in Heaven Above 34
    Glory to God 35
    The Shepherds Were Watching Their Flocks 36
    What Lovely Infant Can This Be 37
The Three Wise Men 38
I'll Be Nice 39
The Little Bird 39
Sleep, My Little Jesus 40
To the Child Jesus 40
A Thousand Stars 41
Frosty Little Snowflakes 41
Our Flag 42
Hail to George Washington 42
There Are Many Flags in Many Lands 43
Our Lady's Children 44
I Will Give Glory to Thee 45
Cradle Song 45
Softly I Rock You 46
God Made This Lovely Earth 46

Lent and Passiontide
Jesus, in The Bitter Sorrow 47
Parce Domine 47
At the Cross Her Station Keeping 48
Infant Jesus 48
However Early I May Be 49
Morning Prayer 50
God's Stars 50
Hail, Holy Joseph, Hail 51
The Child's Star 51
Saint Patrick 52
Six Little Mice 53
Loving Care 54

Eastertide
Alleluia 54
Ye Sons and Daughters of the Lord 54
Easter Bells 55
O Heavenly Queen (Regina Coeli) 55
Easter 56
The Robin's Song 56
On Easter Day 57
The Annunciation 57
Little Baby Brother 58
A Child's Good Night 55

Contents

Pentecost

Holy Spirit, Be My Light 51
To the Trinity 51
My Little House 52
Blessed Be God 53
Chants to Our Lady 53
Holy Mary, Blessed Mary 54
Dancing Long Ago 55
Minuet In F 56
Come, Dear Jesus 57
Lullaby, Little Jesus 58
Little Things 58
Adios, Reina del Cielo 58
My Country 59
Saint Francis and the Wolf (Play with Music) 60
We Sing the Mass 70

We Sing the Mass

The Offertory 71
The Preface 71
Sanctus 71
Benedictus 72
The Communion 72
Agnus Dei 73

DEDICATION

*This book is dedicated
to all children
in honor of the Holy Family*

After Pentecost

Sing unto the Lord a new song, because He has done wonderful things.

Psalm 97

God, Our Loving Father

RICHARD COMPTON FINNISH MELODY

1. Who made o-cean, earth and sky? God, our lov-ing Fa-ther.
2. Who made lakes and riv-ers too? God, our lov-ing Fa-ther.

Who made sun and moon on high? God, our lov-ing Fa-ther.
Who made snow and rain and dew? God, our lov-ing Fa-ther.

Who made all the birds that fly? God, our lov-ing Fa-ther.
Who made lit-tle chil-dren too? God, our lov-ing Fa-ther.

When I Look at the Sky

SISTER JOHN JOSEPH, C.S.J.

1. When I look at the sky in the morn-ing, I say, "Oh, how fine it will be."
2. When I look at the sky in the eve-ning, I say, "Thank You, Lord, for this day."

And I ask dear-est Moth-er — Ma - ry To look and to smile on me.
And I ask Him to look with — mer - cy On all that I did to - day.

Sing the whole song with music names.

Maiden Mother, Meek and Mild

Words from ROMAN HYMNAL   TWELFTH CENTURY MELODY

1. Maid-en Moth-er, meek and mild, take, oh take me for thy child,
2. Teach me when the sun-beam bright calls me with its gold-en light,
3. When my eyes are closed in sleep, through the night my slum-bers keep.

All my life, oh, let it be my best joy to think of thee,
How my wak-ing thoughts may be turned to Je - sus and to thee,
Make my lat - est thought to be how to love thy Son and thee,

Vir - go Ma - ri - a.
Vir - go Ma - ri - a.
Vir - go Ma - ri - a.

Moon

MATTHIAS BARR | FRANZ JOSEPH HAYDN

Clap once for a quarter note. (♩) Clap twice for a half note. (𝅗𝅥)
Clap three times for a dotted-half note. (𝅗𝅥.)

The Stars

SISTER JEANNE MARIE, C.S.J. | SISTER ROSE MARGARET, C.S.J.

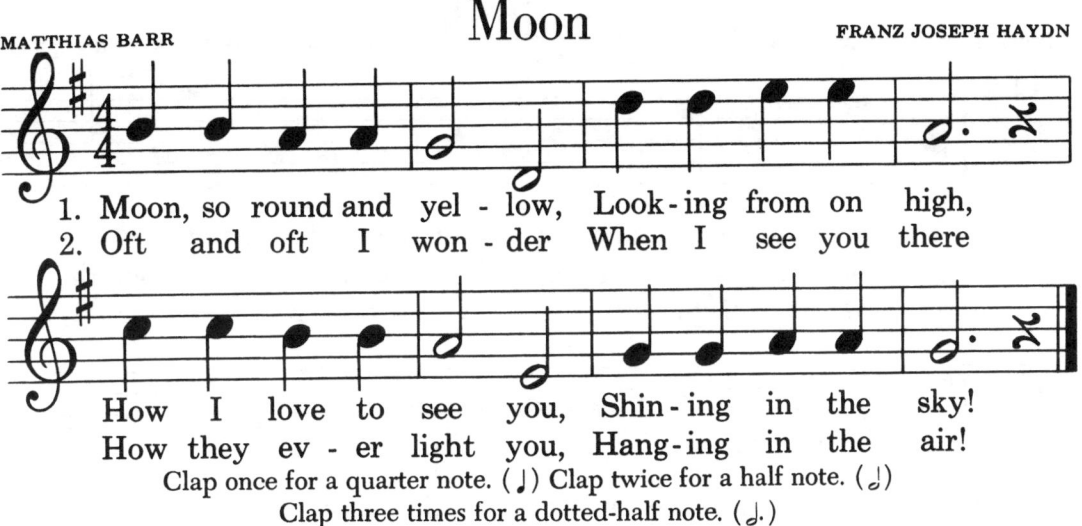

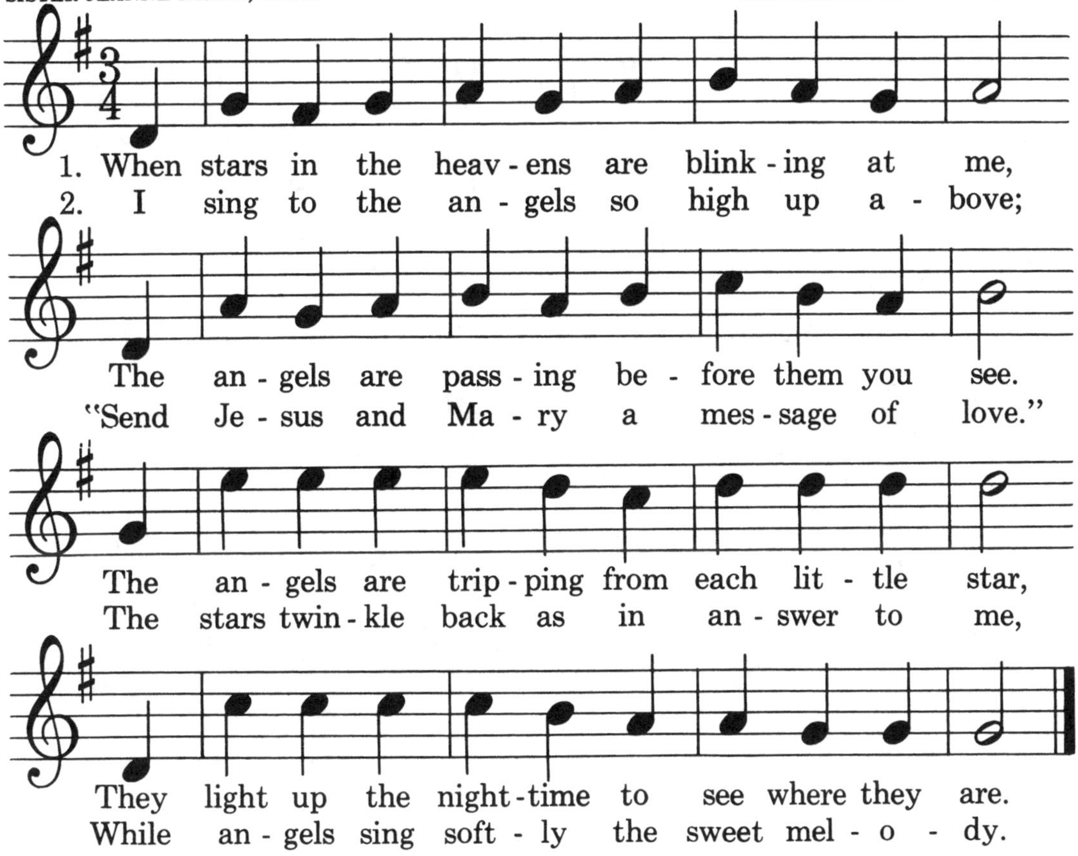

Gratitude

SISTER M. IMMACULATA, S.S.J.   SISTER ROSE MARGARET, C.S.J.

1. I heard a small bird sing-ing When day had closed her eyes.
2. I saw a flow-er clos-ing Its pet-als soft and white,
3. I saw a small child pray-ing, A moth-er sweet and mild,

"God is good," sang the bird-ling, "So good," sang the skies.
"God is good," sang the flow-er, "So good," sang the night.
"God is good," sang the moth-er, "So good," sang the child.

Sleepy Song

ANONYMOUS

1. Lull-a-by, lull-a-by, Do not wake and weep,
2. Lull-a-by, lull-a-by, Lov-ing watch we keep,

Soft-ly in the cra-dle lie, Sleep, O sleep;
Soft-ly in the cra-dle lie, Sleep, O sleep;

Soft-ly in the cra-dle lie, Sleep, O sleep.
Soft-ly in the cra-dle lie, Sleep, O sleep.

Sing this song with music names.

Raise Our Flag

English version by
CAROL FULLER

HUNGARIAN FOLK SONG

1. Raise our flag, love-ly flag! Up-ward watch it go!
2. Shad-ows fall, touch-ing all; Now through sun-set light,

Col-ors bright in morn-ing glow, Wav-ing joy to all be-low.
Drop-ping slow-ly down to rest, Like a bird that finds her nest,

See our flag, love-ly flag! Bu-gle, bu-gle blow!
Comes our flag, love-ly flag! Bu-gle calls, "Good night!"

Try to sing this whole song with music names.

Timothy's Flute

Tim-o-thy toots his lit-tle tin flute. Tim-o-thy plays a tune,

G G B B G A A D D E D G.

13

Indian Hunter

MARK NOLAN

1. In-dian Hunt-er, where are you go-ing, Dash-ing o'er the prai-rie wide?
2. Where the prai-rie grass is— wav-ing There are herds of buf-fa-lo
3. There are hun-gry mouths in the wig-wam. I must find some food to eat.

Fast-er than the fly-ing— ar-row, Tell me where you ride?
Wait-ing for my fly-ing— ar-row And my sing-ing bow.
Hunt-ing o'er the wide, wide prai-rie, I shall bring them meat.

A measure is the music between two bar lines.
How many measures are there in this song?

Are You Sleeping?

OLD FRENCH ROUND

Are you sleep-ing, are you sleep-ing, Broth-er John, Broth-er John?
Frè-re Jac-ques, Frè-re Jac-ques, dor-mez-vous, dor-mez-vous?

Morn-ing bells are ring-ing, morn-ing bells are ring-ing,
Son-nez les ma-ti-nes, son-nez les ma-ti-nes,

"Ding, ding, dong, ding, ding, dong."
Din, din, don, din, din, don!

You can learn to sing this song in French.

Lights

HOPE ANN RHODES

SPANISH FOLK TUNE

If you tap all the notes and rests correctly, how many times will you tap in each measure?

Telling Time

NANCY BYRD TURNER

ARGENTINE FOLK TUNE

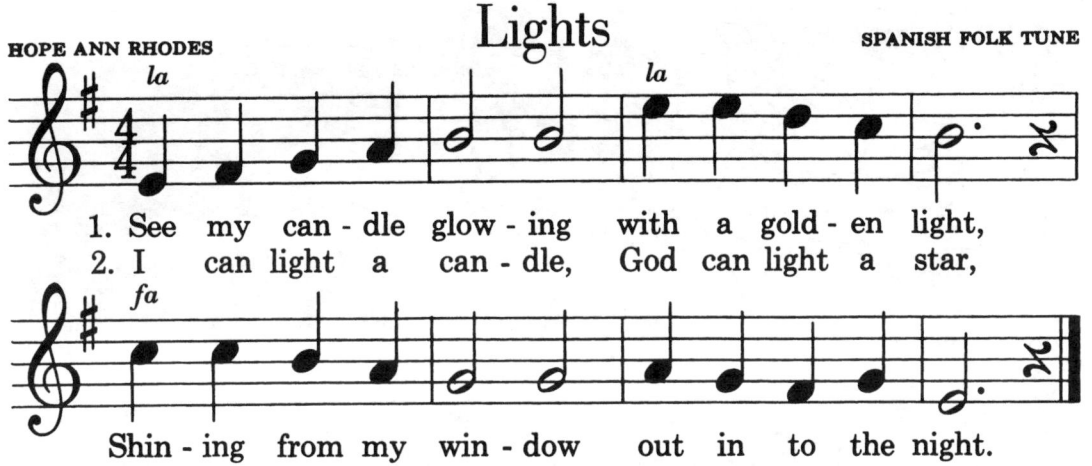

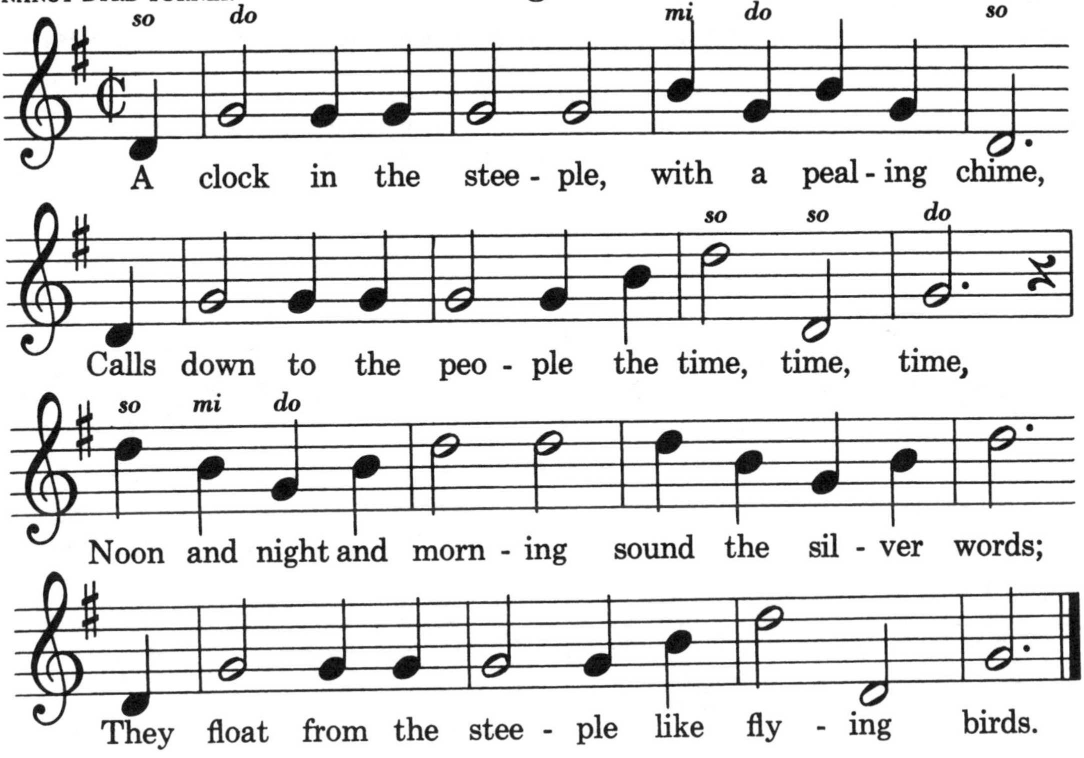

Sing all of this song with music names.
You can play it on your flutes.

My Angel

MARYBETH BAYLEY — POLISH

do so

Lit-tle an-gel, hear me pray; Guard me, watch me all the day.
By my side when night grows deep, Bless and keep me while I sleep.

The two numbers at the beginning of a song are called a time signature.
The upper number tells you how many times to count in each measure.
In this song, how many times do you count in a measure?

Dear Angel Ever at My Side

WILLIAM FABER — ENGLISH

1. Dear an-gel ev-er at my side, How lov-ing must thou be,
2. Thy beau-ti-ful and shin-ing face I see not, though so near,
3. And when I pray, thou pray-est too, Thy pray'r is all for me;

To leave thy home in Heav'n to guard A lit-tle child like me.
The sweet-ness of thy soft, low voice I am too deaf to hear.
But when I sleep, thou sleep-est not, But watch-est pa-tient-ly.

The Golden Rule is the Rule of Three,
It really means God, and my neighbor, and me.
Annette Wynne

St. Francis of Assisi

SISTER ST. AUBYN, C.S.J.   LORRAINE ERICKSON

1. St. Francis loved the wind and rain, He loved each little flower;
2. St. Francis found great peace and joy In doing things for others.

He loved the sunshine and the storms Because they show God's power.
He called the little birds and beasts His sisters and his brothers.

God's Darkness

JOHN MARTIN   SISTER CATHERINE ANTON, C.S.J.

1. God made the dark so day-time could close its weary eyes
2. God made the dark for children and birdies in their nest,

And sleep a while in comfort beneath the starry skies.
All in the dark He watches and guards us while we rest.

Sing all of this song with *so-fa* syllables.

To the King of ages, immortal and invisible, to the Only God, be honor and glory for ever and ever.

Christ, King of Glory

Christ, King of glo-ry, Christ, King of na-tions, Christ, the King of Kings.
Chris-tus vin-cit, Chris-tus re-gnat, Chris-tus im-per-at.

Thou on-ly, O Lord, art ho-ly, to Thee only be power now and for-ev-er.

Christ, King of glo-ry, Christ, King of na-tions, Christ, the King of Kings.
Chris-tus vin-cit, Chris-tus re-gnat, Chris-tus im-per-at.

Father, We Praise You

SISTER RITA ANN, S.C.   GREGORIAN MELODY

1. Fa-ther, we praise You for ev-'ry joy-ful thing,
2. Fa-ther, O make me Your lov-ing child and true,

That fills the world with hap-pi-ness in au-tumn or in spring.
That all Your world may hap-pier be be-cause I'm in it too.

Saint Martin

MARY T. SYNON

WOLFGANG A. MOZART
Arranged

1. Saint — Mar-tin wore a splen-did cloak Which his great king had cho-sen,
2. Saint — Mar-tin cut his cloak in two, To — give half to his broth-er,

But — just out-side the cit - y gate, He met a man half fro - zen.
He — said, "I am a child of God And this man is my broth-er."

St. Martin's Day and Veterans' Day are observed on November 11.
St. Martin was a soldier.

Our Country's Banner

MARYBETH BAYLEY

1. I love to see our coun-try's ban-ner Wav-ing in the morn-ing light,
2. The red is for our he-roes brave Who gave their lives for me and you,
3. And when you see the shin-ing stars, The snow-y stripes so pure and white,

I love to see its twin-kling stars, Its stripes of red and white.
The blue is for their loy - al - ty, For they were ev - er true.
Re - mem-ber you must al - ways keep Your hon - or clean and bright.

Tap once for every quarter note.
How many times must you tap in each measure?

Little Bunnies

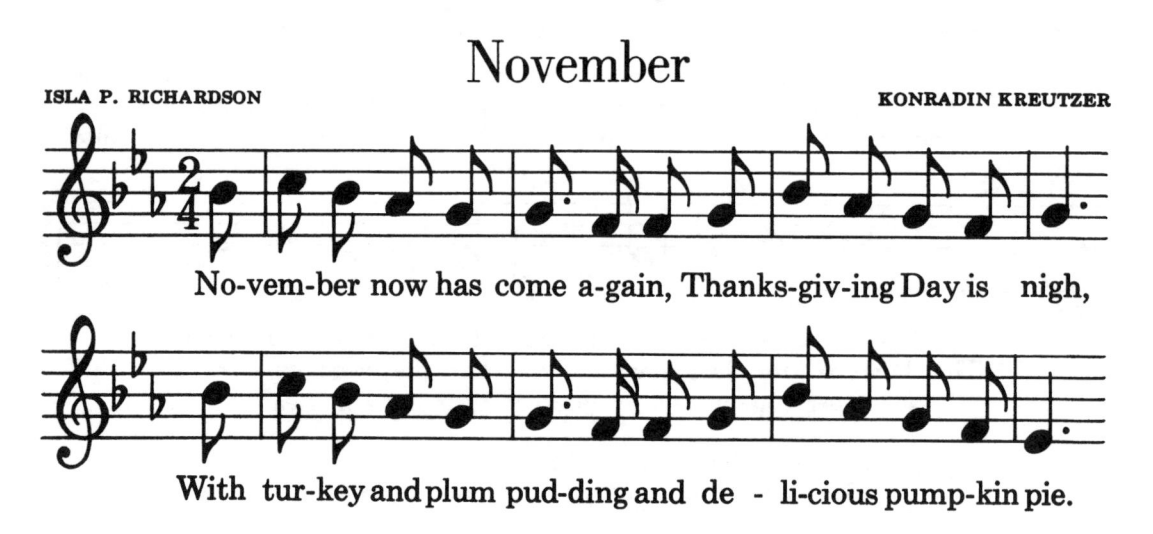

SISTER JOHN JOSEPH, C.S.J.

O-ver the fields with a lip-pe-ty lop,
The dear lit-tle bun-nies go hip-pe-ty hop.
Run, run, bun-nies, there's a man with a gun;
And in-to their holes the bun-nies will pop.

November

ISLA P. RICHARDSON
KONRADIN KREUTZER

No-vem-ber now has come a-gain, Thanks-giv-ing Day is nigh,
With tur-key and plum pud-ding and de-li-cious pump-kin pie.

What fun we have at grand-ma's house, we laugh and romp and play,

We al-ways have such hap-py times up-on Thanks-giv-ing Day.

The earth is full of the goodness of the Lord.

Father, We Thank Thee

AUTHOR UNKNOWN　　　　　　　　　　　　　　OLD RUSSIAN FOLK TUNE

Not too fast

1. Fa - ther, we thank Thee for the night
2. Help us to do the things we should,

And for the pleas - ant morn - ing light,
To be to oth - ers kind and good,

For home and food and lov - ing care
In all we do, in all we say,

And all that makes the day so fair.
To grow more lov - ing ev - 'ry day.

21

Advent

Make ready the way of the Lord, make straight His paths.
Isaias

Come, Lord Jesus

SISTER CECILIA, S.C.

Come, Lord Je-sus, come from heav-en, All the world is wait-ing for Thee.

Son of God and Son of Ma-ry, Low we bow our heads be-fore Thee.

The Advent Wreath

JAN BEZDEK

1. Just four more weeks 'til Christ-mas! The day when Christ our Lord was born.
2. Just three more weeks 'til Christ-mas! We'll say our pray'rs and sing our hymn,
3. Just two more weeks 'til Christ-mas! When lit-tle Je-sus comes to us.
4. Just one more week 'til Christ-mas! Our Sav-ior will be with us soon.

Our Ad-vent wreath is fresh and green With one white can-dle all a-glow!
Then wait to see our Ad-vent wreath With two white can-dles all a-glow!
Our Ad-vent wreath looks bright and green With three white can-dles all a-glow!
We're gath-ered 'round our Ad-vent wreath, Its four white can-dles all a-glow!

Do you have an Advent wreath in your home?

Veni, Domine

Ve - ni, Do - mi - ne Je - su, Ve - ni, Do

Ve - ni, ve - ni, ve - ni, et no - li tar - da - re.

O Come, O Come, Emmanuel

O come, O come, Em - man - u - el,

And ran - som cap - tive Is - ra - el,

That mourns in lone-ly ex - ile here, Un-til the Son of God __ ap-pear.

Re-joice! Re-joice! O Is - ra - el, To thee shall come Em-man-u-el.

Mary, Our Mother

SISTER JOHN JOSEPH, C.S.J.

Ma - ry, most ho - ly, Ma - ry, so mild;
Moth - er of Je - sus, sweet Ho - ly Child.
Moth - er of sin - ners, hear those who call;
Moth - er of chil - dren, Moth - er of all.

Sing a whole line on one breath.

Sunday and Monday

MORSE-McCARTHY WILSON WHITE

do fa re ti so do

1. On Sun-day, on Sun-day, I try to be so ver-y, ver-y good;
2. On Mon-day, on Mon-day, I'm not so good, no mat-ter how I try;

That's one day, that's one day, I do just what I should.
But Sun-day, but Sun-day, Oh, who's so good as I?

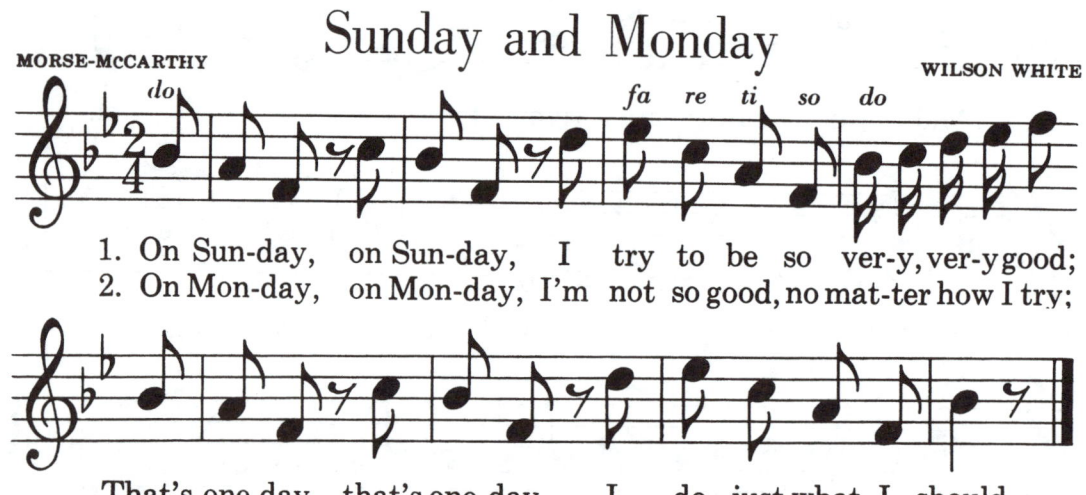

Christmastide and After

This day you shall know that the Lord is coming and tomorrow you shall see His glory.

Introit for the Vigil of Christmas

O Come, All Ye Faithful (Adeste Fideles)

F. OAKELEY   OLD LATIN

O come, all ye faith-ful, Joy-ful and tri-um-phant,
O come ye, O come ye to Beth-le-hem;
Come and be-hold Him, Born the King of An-gels;
O come, let us a-dore Him, O come, let us a-dore Him,
O come, let us a-dore Him, Christ, the Lord.

Christ Was Born in Bethlehem

YUGOSLAVIAN CAROL

1. Christ was born in Beth-le-hem, Let us all re-joice.
2. Christ was born in Beth-le-hem, Let us all re-joice.

Praise to God the an-gels sing. Peace and joy to all we bring.
Chil-dren, all be glad and sing, 'Tis the birth-day of your King.

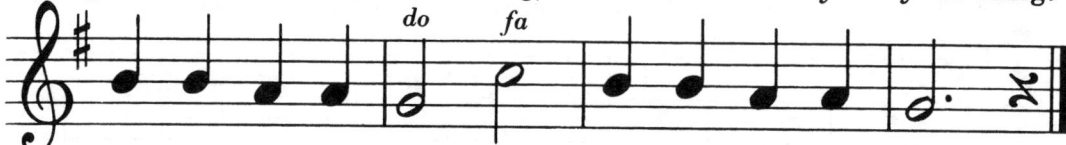

Come, let us a-dore Him, Come, let us a-dore.
Come, let us a-dore Him, Come, let us a-dore.

Only the difficult syllables are written in. You can read the others by yourselves.

I Saw Three Ships

ENGLISH CAROL

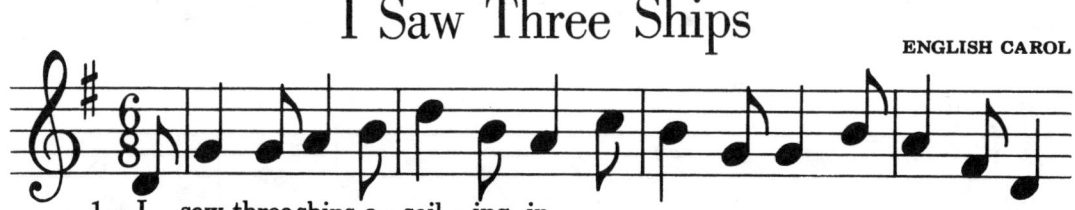

1. I saw three ships a-sail-ing in,
2. And who came sail-ing in those ships?
3. The ho-ly Vir-gin and her Son,   On Christ-mas Day, on Christ-mas Day,
4. Then let us all re-joice and sing,

I saw three ships a-sail-ing in,
And who came sail-ing in those ships?
The ho-ly Vir-gin and her Son,   On Christ-mas Day in the morn-ing.
Then let us all re-joice and sing,

Our Lady Came to Bethlehem

SISTER CECILIA, S.C.

1. Our La-dy came to Beth-le-hem when all the stars were bright.
2. A-long the road to Beth-le-hem St. Jo-seph led the way.

The shep-herds on the hill-side watched their lambs all snow-y white.
He found the sta-ble on the hill, the gos-pel sto-ries say,

Our La-dy knew the Lamb of God would come be-fore the morn-ing light,
And for the lit-tle Lamb of God, He made a bed of soft-est hay,

And she would hold Him in her arms that hap-py Christ-mas night.
He held the Sav-ior in his arms that hap-py Christ-mas Day.

Hasten, O Shepherds

TRANSLATED — SPANISH FOLK SONG

Has-ten, O shep-herds, has-ten. Come to Beth-le-hem.
Va-mos, pas-to-res, va-mos, Va-mos, a Be-lén,

See the Ho-ly In-fant, The glo-rious Son of God.
A ver a-quel Ni-ño, La glo-ria Dios le dé.

Perhaps you could learn this song in Spanish.

Winds Through the Olive Trees

ANONYMOUS — S. C.

mi

1. Winds through the ol-ive trees soft-ly did blow,
2. Then from the star-ry sky an-gels bent low

'Round lit-tle Beth-le-hem long, long a-go.
Sing-ing their song of love, long, long a-go.

Sheep on the hill-side lay whit-er than snow,
For in a man-ger bed cra-dled we know,

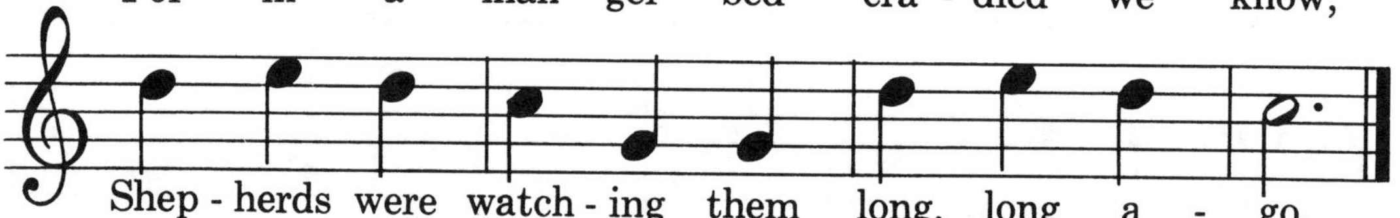

Shep-herds were watch-ing them long, long a-go.
Christ came to Beth-le-hem long, long a-go.

Which phrases are alike and which are different?

28

The Christ Child

ITALIC: ITALIAN

so

1. When Jesus came to earth one night,
2. O Jesus, from Your bed of hay,

The angels sang, the stars were bright,
Give me Your blessing as I pray,

la   fa   re

For He was King of love and light.
That I may love You more each day,

The angels sang, the stars were bright.
Give me Your blessing as I pray.

Which phrases are alike?

A Christmas Wish

SISTER M. JOSITA, O.S.F.   ENGLISH CHRISTMAS CAROL

1. I wish I could have been on earth When Mary came to Bethlehem,
2. If only I had been on earth That time so many years ago,

And Joseph went from house to house To find a shelt'ring home for them.
I would have opened wide my door To shelter Jesus from the cold.

29

MY GIFT

What can I give Him,
  Small that I am?
If I were a shepherd
  I would bring a lamb.
If I were a wise man
  I would do my part;
Yet what I can, I give Him;
  Give Him my heart.
  Christina G. Rossetti

Oh, Come Little Children

TRANSLATED J.P.A. SCHULZ

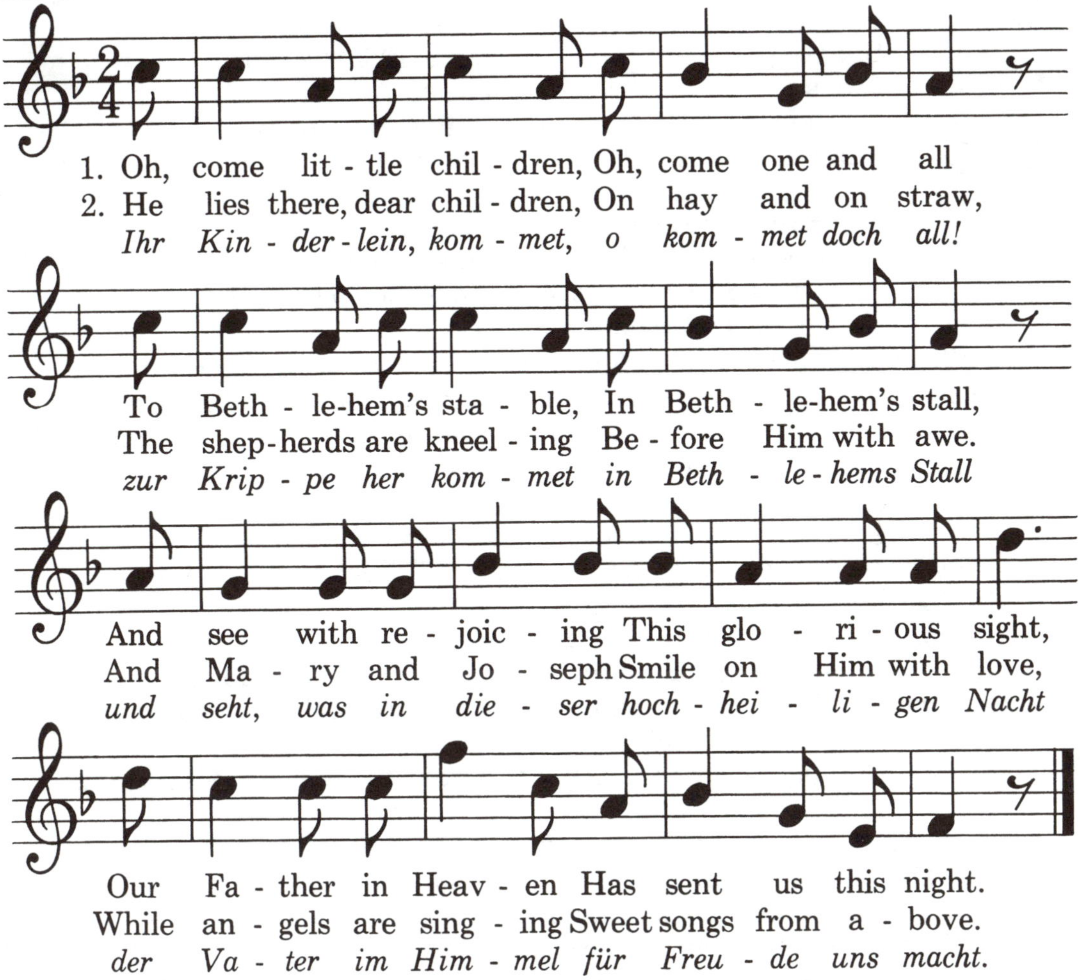

1. Oh, come little children, Oh, come one and all
2. He lies there, dear children, On hay and on straw,
Ihr Kin-der-lein, kom-met, o kom-met doch all!

To Bethlehem's stable, In Bethlehem's stall,
The shepherds are kneeling Before Him with awe.
zur Krip-pe her kom-met in Beth-le-hems Stall

And see with rejoicing This glorious sight,
And Mary and Joseph Smile on Him with love,
und seht, was in die-ser hoch-hei-li-gen Nacht

Our Father in Heaven Has sent us this night.
While angels are singing Sweet songs from above.
der Va-ter im Him-mel für Freu-de uns macht.

Perhaps you can learn to sing the German words too.

THE FIRST CHRISTMAS
The Players

St. Joseph	Second Little Angel
Mary	First Shepherd
Simon	Second Shepherd
Jacob	Other Angels
Innkeeper	Other Shepherds
First Little Angel	Choir

Scene 1   A street in Bethlehem.
Scene 2   Just inside the gates of heaven.
Scene 3   Outside the stable in Bethlehem.
Scene 4   Inside the stable.

(*To the center of the front of the classroom a nativity scene, with a manger, is ready. It may be screened until it is needed. To the right, three children represent the houses in Bethlehem. To the left, two angels represent the gates of heaven.*)

Scene 1.
(*A street in Bethlehem.*)

(*Offstage the* Choir *sings the first stanza of "Silent Night."* Mary *and* St. Joseph *enter right.*)

St. Joseph. Mary, here we are at Bethlehem.
Mary. Do you think our cousin, Simon, will have room for us?
St. Joseph. I am sure he will. You wait here while I knock at the door. (*He knocks at the first door.*)
Simon. (*Opening the door.*) Joseph, it is good to see you. What can I do for you?
St. Joseph. May we stay here with you tonight?
Simon. I am sorry Joseph, but we have no room. If you had come a little sooner you could have stayed here.
St. Joseph. Thank you, Simon. (*To* Mary) I'll try Jacob. He is always glad to see us. (*He knocks at the second door.*)

32

JACOB. Good evening, Joseph. I am happy to see you.
ST. JOSEPH. May we stay here with you tonight, Jacob?
JACOB. It is too bad, but our house is already filled. Did you try the inn? You might find room there.
ST. JOSEPH. Thank you, Jacob. (*To* MARY) There is no room here. We might try the inn.
MARY. Maybe they would have one little room for us there.
ST. JOSEPH. Here is the inn. I will ask. (ST. JOSEPH *knocks at the door of the inn.*) Do you have a place for us to stay tonight?
INNKEEPER. (*Gruffly*) We are already crowded. No room!
ST. JOSEPH. (*Sadly*) Mary, I cannot find a place anywhere. What shall we do? (*Short pause*) Mary, there is a stable nearby. Would you mind staying there for tonight?
MARY. No, Joseph. It will be very quiet there. Let us go at once.
ST. JOSEPH. How good you are, Mary! You never complain when things are hard!

(MARY AND JOSEPH *walk off stage.*)

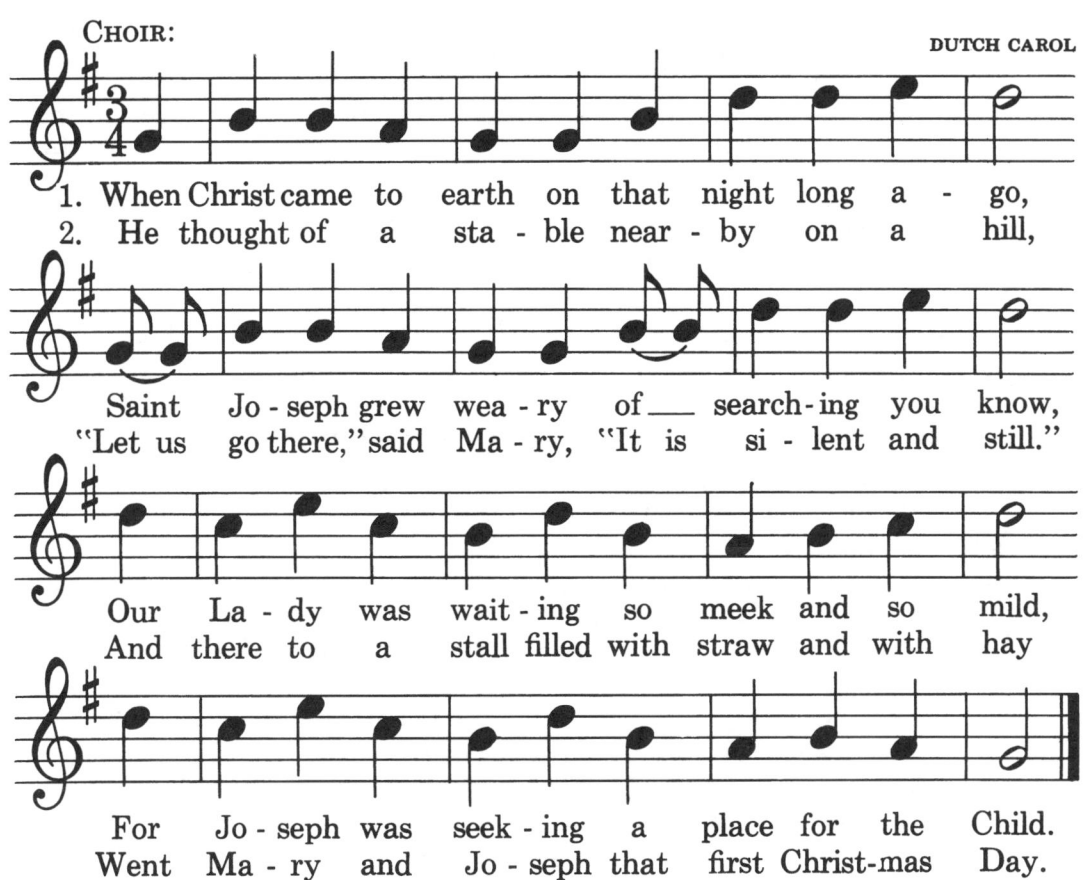

CHOIR:　　　　　　　　　　　　　　　　　　　　　　DUTCH CAROL

1. When Christ came to earth on that night long ago,
   Saint Joseph grew weary of searching you know,
   Our Lady was waiting so meek and so mild,
   For Joseph was seeking a place for the Child.
2. He thought of a stable nearby on a hill,
   "Let us go there," said Mary, "It is silent and still."
   And there to a stall filled with straw and with hay
   Went Mary and Joseph that first Christmas Day.

Scene 2.
(Just inside the gates of heaven.)

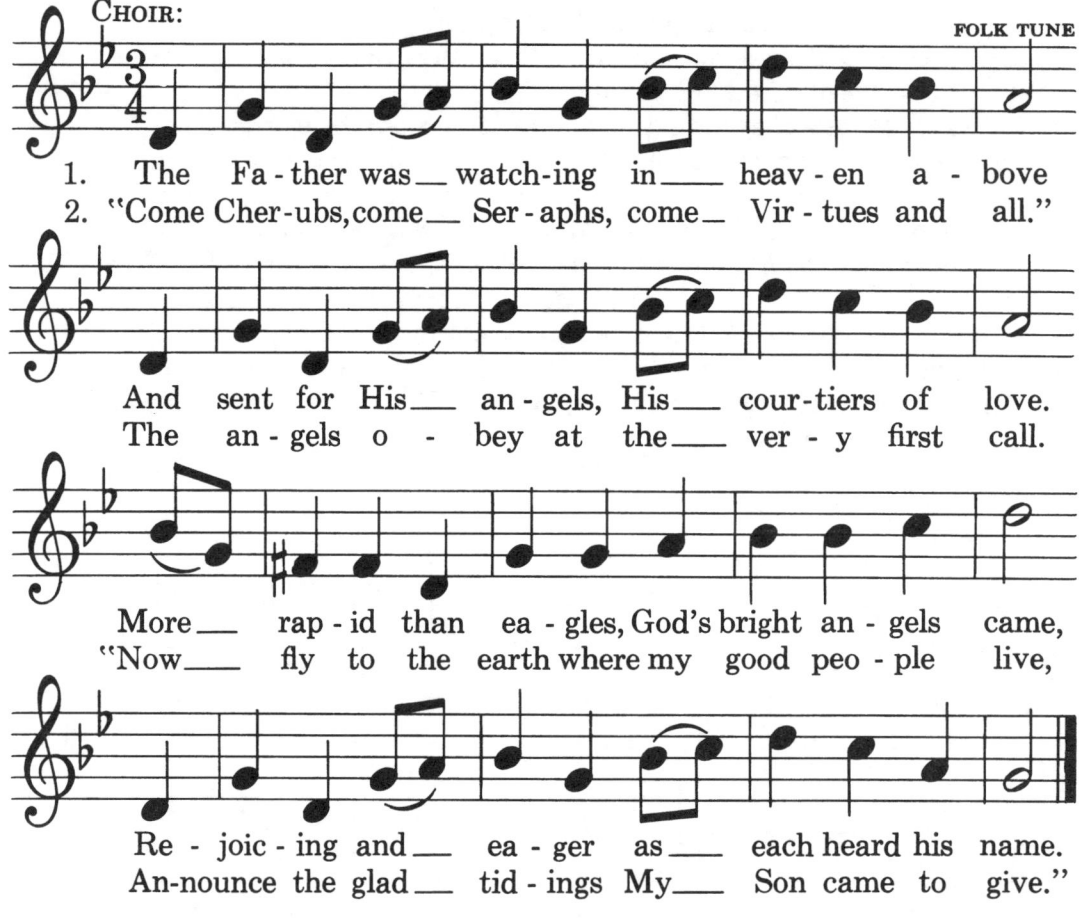

CHOIR: FOLK TUNE

1. The Father was watching in heaven above
And sent for His angels, His courtiers of love.
More rapid than eagles, God's bright angels came,
Rejoicing and eager as each heard his name.

2. "Come Cherubs, come Seraphs, come Virtues and all."
The angels obey at the very first call.
"Now fly to the earth where my good people live,
Announce the glad tidings My Son came to give."

(The front of the room, to the left, may represent the court of heaven. Two little ANGELS are standing within the gates of heaven.)

FIRST ANGEL. Did you hear the wonderful news?

SECOND ANGEL. No! What is it?

FIRST ANGEL. God has just sent for the choirs of angels!

SECOND ANGEL. Why did He do that?

FIRST ANGEL. He wants them to go down to earth and tell the people that the Savior is born.

SECOND ANGEL. There will be a lot of excitement down there on earth when all the people get that good news.

FIRST ANGEL. God didn't send His angels to all the people. He just told them to tell some poor shepherds who are watching their sheep. Look at them on that little hill near Bethlehem!

Second Angel. Listen! We can hear what the angels are singing.
(Angels *backstage are singing.*)

Glory to God

Glo-ry to God and peace on earth, Glo-ry to God on high,

Glo-ry to God we sing to-day, Glo-ry to God.

First Angel. Look! The shepherds are afraid! One of the angels is speaking.

Angel's Voice. Fear not; for, behold, I bring you good tidings of great joy, that shall be to all the people: For, this day, is born to you a Savior, who is Christ the Lord, in the city of David. And this shall be a sign unto you. You shall find the Infant wrapped in swaddling clothes and laid in a manger.

Second Angel. Now the angels are coming back. I wonder if the shepherds will believe. Sometimes men do not believe what we angels tell them.

Scene 3.
(Outside the stable in Bethlehem)

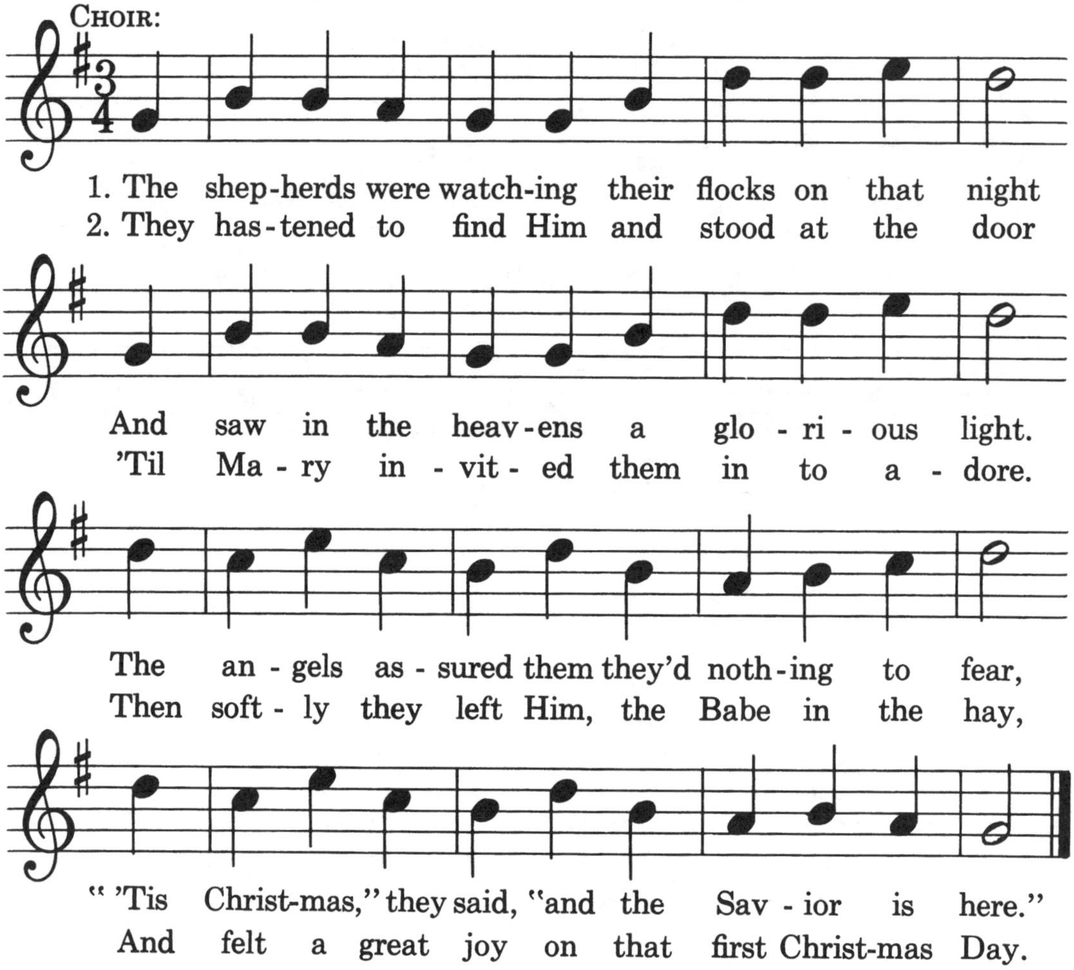

1. The shep-herds were watch-ing their flocks on that night
2. They has-tened to find Him and stood at the door

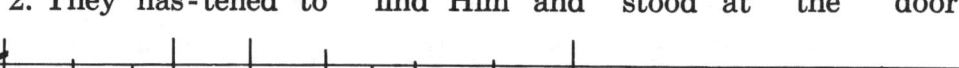

And saw in the heav-ens a glo-ri-ous light.
'Til Ma-ry in-vit-ed them in to a-dore.

The an-gels as-sured them they'd noth-ing to fear,
Then soft-ly they left Him, the Babe in the hay,

" 'Tis Christ-mas," they said, "and the Sav-ior is here."
And felt a great joy on that first Christ-mas Day.

FIRST SHEPHERD. This is all I have to give the Infant Savior—a little white lamb.
SECOND SHEPHERD. The Savior is King of heaven and earth! He needs not our gifts! What He really wants is our love!
FIRST SHEPHERD. Do you think this is the place?
SECOND SHEPHERD. Didn't the angel say we would find the Savior in a stable? There is a light. Maybe this is where we will find Him.
FIRST SHEPHERD. Think how many years we have waited for God to redeem us! But surely He would not be in such a poor place!
SECOND SHEPHERD. Remember the angel's words: "This shall be a sign for you—an Infant wrapped in swaddling clothes and laid in a manger." Let us go in and see.

Scene 4.
(Inside the stable.)

(*The* SHEPHERDS *enter. While they offer their gifts the* CHOIR *sings the second stanza of "Silent Night."*)

(*After they have offered their gifts, they kneel around the crib while all sing "What Lovely Infant Can This Be?"*)

What Lovely Infant Can This Be?

TRADITIONAL

1. What love-ly In-fant can this be, That in the lit-tle crib I see?
2. Who is that La-dy kneel-ing by, And look-ing down with lov-ing eye?

So sweet-ly on the straw It lies, It must have come from par-a-dise,
Oh, that is Ma-ry, ev-er blest, How full of joy her ho-ly breast,

It must have come from par-a-dise.
How full of joy her ho-ly breast.

3. What man is that who seems to smile
And looks so blissful all the while?
The holy Joseph, good and true.
The Infant makes him happy too.

4. And now, what makes the cave so bright,
And who is singing through the night?
Why, they are angels small and fair.
Their songs of joy fill all the air.

5. Those men all kneeling in the hay—
With crooks to lean on—who are they?
Poor shepherds; they were fast asleep
When angels called them from their sheep.

6. Why does the ox bend down so low?
What does the little donkey know?
See how they warm His tiny feet.
Their task is small, but very sweet.

When the wise men saw the star, they said one to another: "This is the sign of the great King: let us go and search for him, and offer him gifts, gold, frankincense, and myrrh."

Antiphon for Epiphany

The Three Wise Men

MARY SMITH   FRENCH CAROL

1. There were three king-ly wise men,
2. 'Twas in the shin-ing star-light,

Who came from far-a-way on Christ-mas Day,
Their shag-gy cam-els trot-ted all the way

To see the lit-tle Sav-ior Sleep-ing on the hay,
To see the lit-tle Sav-ior Sleep-ing on the hay,

Our Sav-ior sleep-ing on the hay.
Our Sav-ior sleep-ing on the hay.

I'll Be Nice

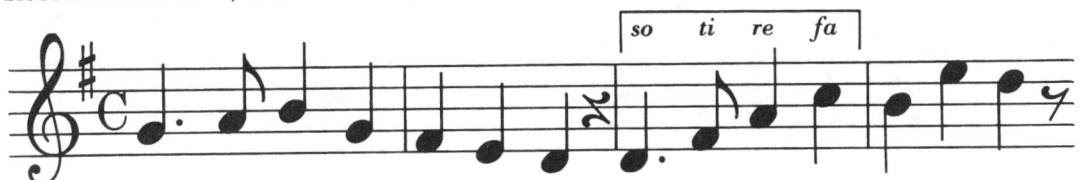

SISTER MIRIAM JANE, S.C.
SISTER CECILIA, S.C.

so ti re fa

la la fa

1. I'll be nice to Bill and Jane, I'll be nice to Ma-ry Lou,
   Be-cause God loves them, so will I, And I will treat them kind-ly too.
2. If there's some-thing I can do, When they're bus-y as can be,
   Be-cause God loves them, so will I, And I will help them cheer-ful-ly.

The Little Bird

REGINA ENNIS
MARIAN HALL

Boys
Did you see the lit-tle bird on your win-dow sill to-day?
Did you hear his lit-tle song, oh so glad and gay?

Girls
Yes, I saw the lit-tle bird and I heard his lit-tle song
And I hope he'll come a-gain on an-oth-er day.

In this song there are many eighth notes. (♫) Last year we called them "running notes."

Tap just once for two eighth notes.

Sleep, My Little Jesus

TRANSLATED
LATVIAN CAROL

1. Sleep, my little Jesus, still and quiet be.
   While You sleep St. Joseph is watching over Thee.
2. Lullaby, sweet Jesus, Mary's rocking Thee.
   When again You waken, her lovely face You'll see.

To the Child Jesus

REV. W. ROCHE
SISTER JOHN JOSEPH, C.S.J.

Dear Child divine, sweet Brother mine, Be with me all the day,

And when the light has turned to night, Be with me still I pray,

Wher-e'er I be, come Thou with me And never go away.

Dear Child divine, sweet Brother mine, Be with me all the day.

A Thousand Stars

ETHEL CROWNINSHIELD
ROBERT SCHUMANN

Softly and not too fast

1. A thou-sand stars up in the sky, Just one shin-ing sun;
2. The day is light, the night is dark, But God nev-er sleeps.

So man-y chil-dren in the world, Yet God knows ev-'ry one.
And o-ver chil-dren ev-'ry-where A lov-ing watch He keeps.

Frosty Little Snowflakes

ST. TERESA'S SCHOOL, ST. LOUIS

1. Frost-y lit-tle snow-flakes fall-ing on the ground,
2. Here's the mer-ry sun-shine com-ing out to play,

Hap-py lit-tle chil-dren play-ing all a-round.
All the fun-ny snow-men start to melt a-way.

Some are mak-ing snow-men, some are mak-ing balls,
Down they go a-tum-bling in the smil-ing sun,

Some are laugh-ing cheer-i-ly as the snow falls.
Not a snow-man will be left when the day's done.

Tap the rhythm of "Frosty Little Snowflakes." There are four eighth notes and two quarter notes. (♪ ♪ ♪ ♪ | ♩ ♩)
How many times can you find this rhythm pattern?

Our Flag

PITTSBURGH SCHOOL CHILDREN

Hats off! Eyes right! The flag pass-es by!

The red and white and blue!

Ban - ner of our coun - try

We'll be true to you!

The red and white and blue!

All the notes in this song are *do, mi* or *so.*

Hail to George Washington

JOHN BARTON

Hail to George Wash-ing-ton! The fa - ther of our coun - try.

First in war and first in peace
And first in the hearts of his coun-try-men.

There Are Many Flags in Many Lands

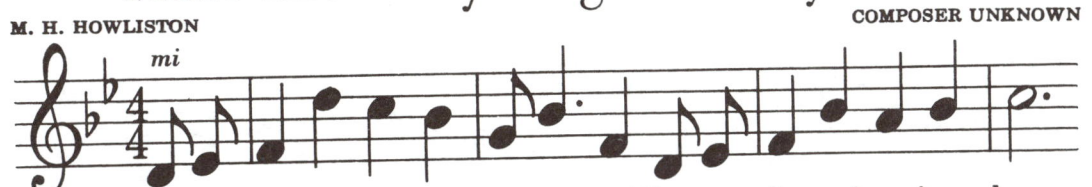

M. H. HOWLISTON COMPOSER UNKNOWN

There are man-y flags in man-y lands, There are flags of ev-'ry hue;
But there is no flag, how-ev-er grand, Like our own Red, White and Blue.

CHORUS
Then hur-rah for the flag, Our coun-try's flag, Its stripes and white stars, too;
There is no flag in an-y land, Like our own Red, White and Blue.

Our Lady's Children

SISTER CECILIA, S.C.

Lit - tle girl from Mex - i - co, Lit - tle boy from Bor - ne - o,

Lit - tle girl from far Ma - lay, Lit - tle boy from U. S. A.

Boys from Chi - na and Ja - pan, Girls from Spain and Switz - er - land,

Boys and girls from far and near Love our Bless - ed Moth - er dear.

I Will Give Glory to Thee

Adapted from a psalm

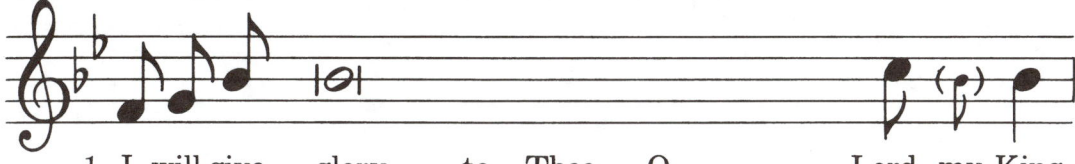

1. I will give glory to Thee, O Lord, my King.
2. I will give glory to Thy name for-ev-er.
3. My soul shall praise Thee, O Lord, for-ev-er.

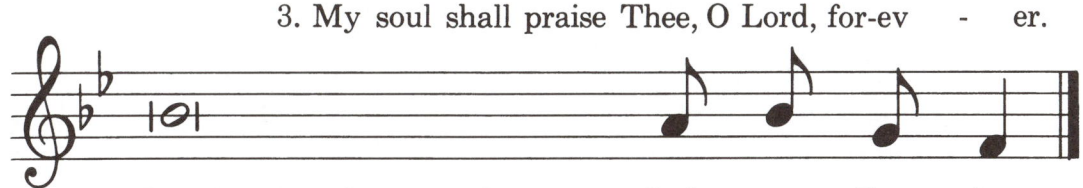

I will praise Thee, O God, my Sav-ior.
for Thou hast been a helper and pro-tec-tor.
Thou hast helped me according to Thy great mer-cy.

Cradle Song

ANONYMOUS   GERMAN FOLK SONG

1. Sleep, ba-by, sleep, Thy fa-ther tends the sheep;
2. Sleep, ba-by, sleep, And you shall have a sheep;

Thy moth-er shakes the dream-land tree And down come all the dreams for thee.
And he shall have a gold-en bell, And play with ba-by in the dell.

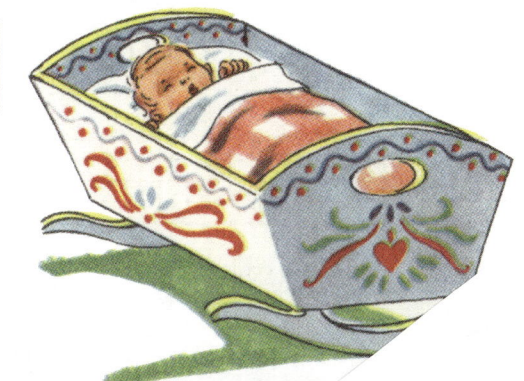

Sleep, ba-by, sleep.
Sleep, ba-by, sleep.

Softly I Rock You

SISTER CECILIA, S.C.   SPANISH FOLK TUNE

1. Soft-ly I rock you, my lit-tle one, sweet-ly I sing you to sleep.
2. An-gels will guard you, my lit-tle one, keep-ing you safe in their care.

All through the night the moon will smile on your slum-ber deep.
An-gels with gold-en wings and stars in their shin-ing hair.

God Made This Lovely Earth

SISTER M. JOSITA, O.S.F.   RUSSIAN FOLK TUNE

1. God made this love-ly earth of ours, Its might-y lands and seas.
2. God made the world of an-gels bright To stand be-fore His throne,

He made the sun, the moon and stars, The blos-soms and the trees.
To sing His love, to do His will, To be His ver-y own.

When you sing the two eighth notes (♫) remember to tap only once.

Lent and Passiontide

Hear us, O God of mercy, and show to our minds the light of Thy grace.
Prayer for Ember Friday of Lent

Jesus, in Thy Bitter Sorrow
SISTER CECILIA, S.C.

Je-sus, in Thy bit-ter sor-row All my sins were laid on Thee.

Nails and spear, and thorns that crowned Thee, All were borne for me.

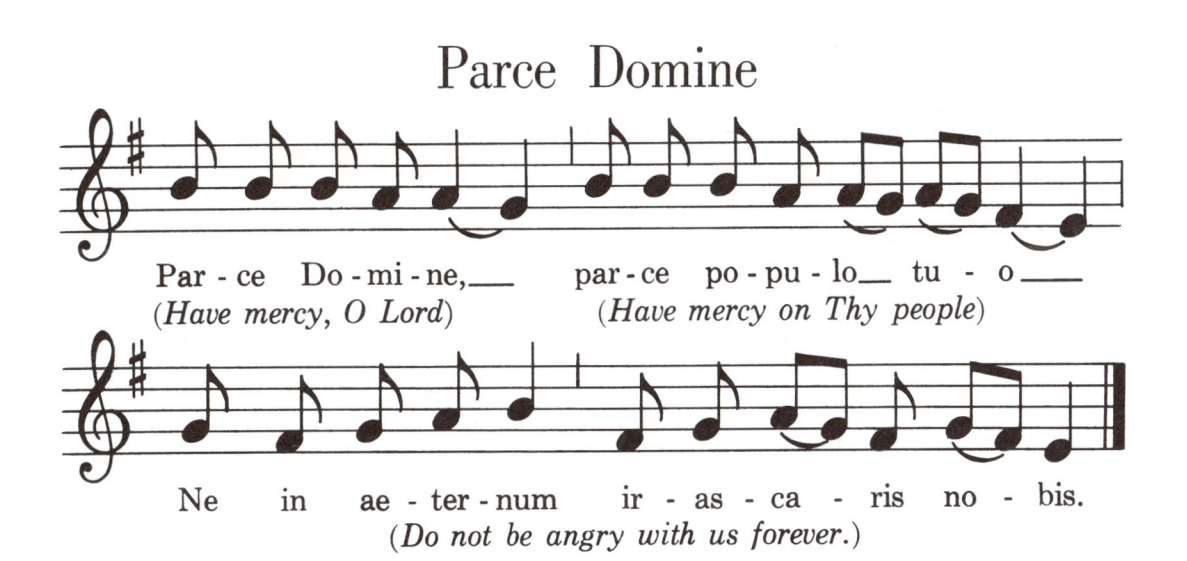

Parce Domine

Par-ce Do-mi-ne, par-ce po-pu-lo tu-o
(Have mercy, O Lord) *(Have mercy on Thy people)*

Ne in ae-ter-num ir-as-ca-ris no-bis.
(Do not be angry with us forever.)

At the Cross Her Station Keeping

TRADITIONAL

1. At the Cross, her sta-tion keep-ing,
Stood the mourn-ful Moth-er weep-ing, Close to Je-sus to the last.
2. Through her heart, His sor-row shar-ing,
All His bit-ter an-guish bear-ing. Now at length the sword has passed.

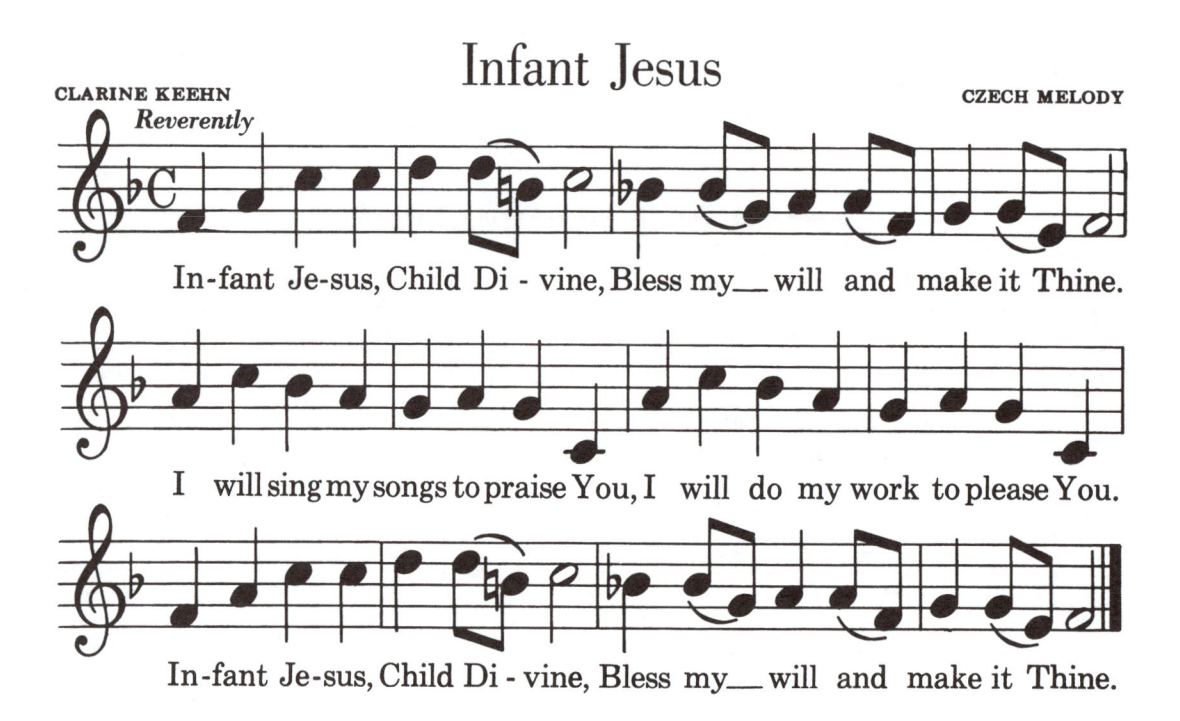

Infant Jesus

CLARINE KEEHN *Reverently*   **CZECH MELODY**

In-fant Je-sus, Child Di-vine, Bless my will and make it Thine.

I will sing my songs to praise You, I will do my work to please You.

In-fant Je-sus, Child Di-vine, Bless my will and make it Thine.

However Early I May Be

DANIEL LORD, S.J. JAN BEZDEK

How - ev - er ear - ly I may be,
The rob - in's up a - head of me.
His break - fast eat - en, pray'rs all said,
And call - ing me a sleep - y head.
But some day soon, I give my word,
I'm going to beat that ear - ly bird.

Morning Prayer

SISTER M. IMMACULATA S.S.J.
SISTER ROSE MARGARET, C.S.J.

1. I woke up one morn-ing and slipped out of bed,
2. "To whom are you sing-ing, dear bird-ie," said I,

For close to my win-dow, just o-ver my head,
"While ev-er you're look-ing up in-to the sky?"

A lit-tle gray spar-row was sing-ing "Tweet-tweet."
The spar-row flew near-er and gave a quick nod,

Oh, I nev-er heard mu-sic so clear and so sweet.
"Say your pray'rs, lit-tle child, I am sing-ing to God."

Some of the phrases in this song are nearly alike. Find the places where they differ.

God's Stars

REGINA ENNIS
MARIAN HALL

1. Be-fore I go to sleep at night I look up at the eve-ning sky
2. I close my eyes, but still I see The bright stars shin-ing down on me.

And see a mil-lion lit-tle lights All twin-kling there so far and high.
They tell me God is good and great, And that He watch-es o-ver me.

Joseph was a workingman,
His hands were firm and strong,
His eyes were clear,
His smile was kind,
His heart had goodness in it.

Hail, Holy Joseph, Hail

OLD HYMN

1. Hail, holy Joseph, hail! Chaste spouse of Mary, hail!
2. Hail, holy Joseph, hail! Prince of the House of God!
3. Hail, holy Joseph, hail! God's choice wert thou alone.

Pure as the lily flow'r In Eden's peaceful vale.
May His best graces be By thy sweet hands bestowed.
To thee the Word made Flesh Was subject as a Son!

The Child's Star

JOHN TABB — FOLK TUNE

do mi ... la la fa fa so

1. The star that watched you in your sleep Has just put out his light.
2. But tell the baby when he wakes To watch for my return;

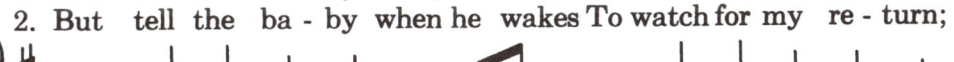

"Good day to you on earth," he said, "Is here in heav'n good night."
For I'll hang out my lamp again When his begins to burn.

The two lines begin alike. Do they end alike?

51

Saint Patrick

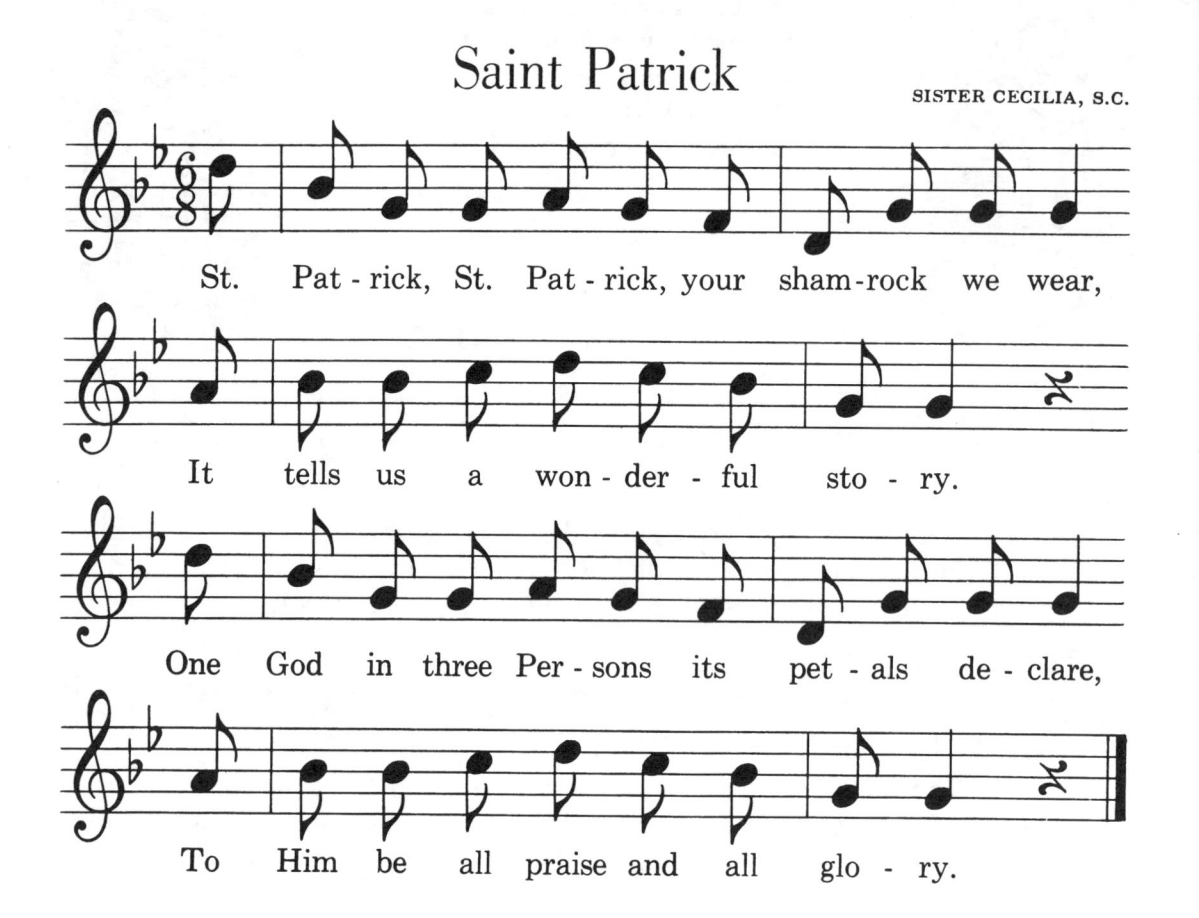

SISTER CECILIA, S.C.

St. Pat-rick, St. Pat-rick, your sham-rock we wear,
It tells us a won-der-ful sto-ry.
One God in three Per-sons its pet-als de-clare,
To Him be all praise and all glo-ry.

Six Little Mice

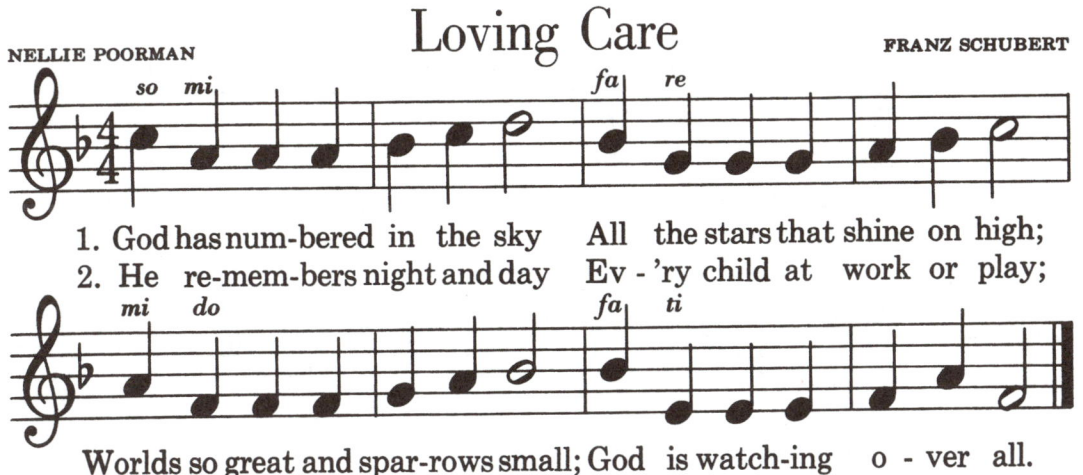

MOTHER GOOSE
ENGLISH FOLK SONG

1. Six lit-tle mice sat down to spin,
2. "Shall I come in and bite off your threads?"

Puss-y passed by and she peeped in,
"Oh no, Miss Puss-y you'll bite off our heads."

"What are you at, my lit-tle men?"
"Oh no, I won't, I'll help you spin."

"Mak-ing good coats for gen-tle-men."
"That may be so, but you can't come in."

Loving Care

NELLIE POORMAN
FRANZ SCHUBERT

so mi ... *fa re*

1. God has num-bered in the sky   All the stars that shine on high;
2. He re-mem-bers night and day   Ev-'ry child at work or play;

mi do ... *fa ti*

Worlds so great and spar-rows small; God is watch-ing o-ver all.
He will teach you what to do; God is watch-ing o-ver you.

53

Eastertide

And very early in the morning, the first day of the week, they came to the sepulchre, the sun being now risen. Alleluia.
Antiphon at Lauds, Easter Vigil

Alleluia

Al - le - lu - ia,   al - le - lu - ia,___ al - le - lu - ia.

Ye Sons and Daughters of the Lord

1,2,3. Al - le - lu - ia,___ al - le - lu - ia,   al - le - lu - ia. (Repeat)

1. Ye sons and daugh-ters of the Lord, The King of glo - ry, King a-dored,
2. On Sun-day morn, at break of day, The faith-ful wom-en went their way,
3. An an - gel clad in white they see, "The Lord ye seek is ris'n," said he,

This day Him-self from death re-stored,   Al - le - lu - ia.   ℟ Alleluia.
To seek the tomb where Je - sus lay,   Al - le - lu - ia.   ℟ Alleluia.
"And goes be - fore to Gal - i - lee,"   Al - le - lu - ia.   ℟ Alleluia.

Easter Bells

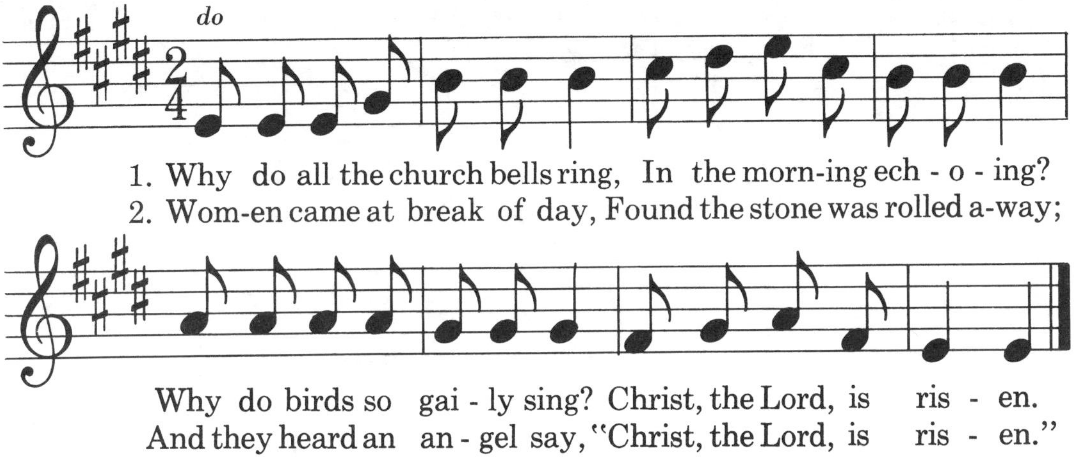

JAMAICAN FOLK TUNE

1. Why do all the church bells ring, In the morning ech-o-ing?
   Why do birds so gai-ly sing? Christ, the Lord, is ris-en.
2. Wom-en came at break of day, Found the stone was rolled a-way;
   And they heard an an-gel say, "Christ, the Lord, is ris-en."

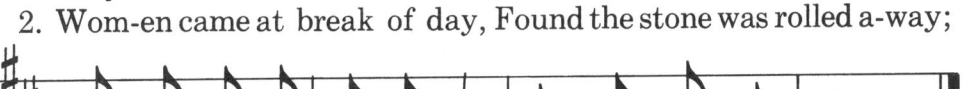

O Heavenly Queen *(Regina Coeli)*

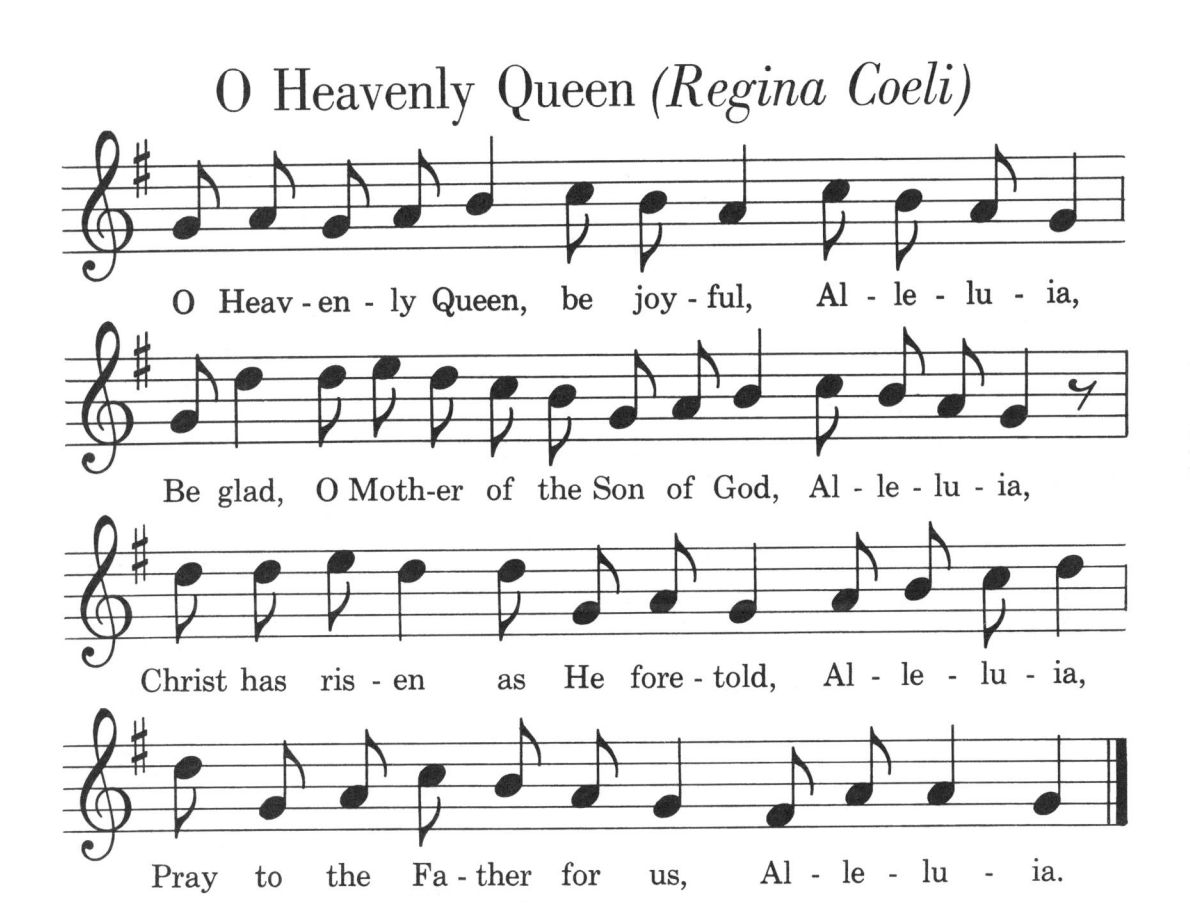

O Heav-en-ly Queen, be joy-ful, Al-le-lu-ia,

Be glad, O Moth-er of the Son of God, Al-le-lu-ia,

Christ has ris-en as He fore-told, Al-le-lu-ia,

Pray to the Fa-ther for us, Al-le-lu-ia.

Easter

DANIEL GOTTLIEB TUERK
Arranged

1. Did the birds on East-er morn Sing with sweet ac-cord?
2. Did the flow-ers raise their heads When He passed their way?

Do you think the trees bowed down To greet our ris-en Lord?
Do you think our La-dy smiled To see her Son that day?

The Robin's Song

S. R. M.

One swing to a measure

"Cheer up," calls the rob-in so sweet and clear;

I hear him sing in the mead-ow near.

"Cheer up," sings he in a gay lit-tle song,

For spring-time has come and win-ter is gone.

On Easter Day

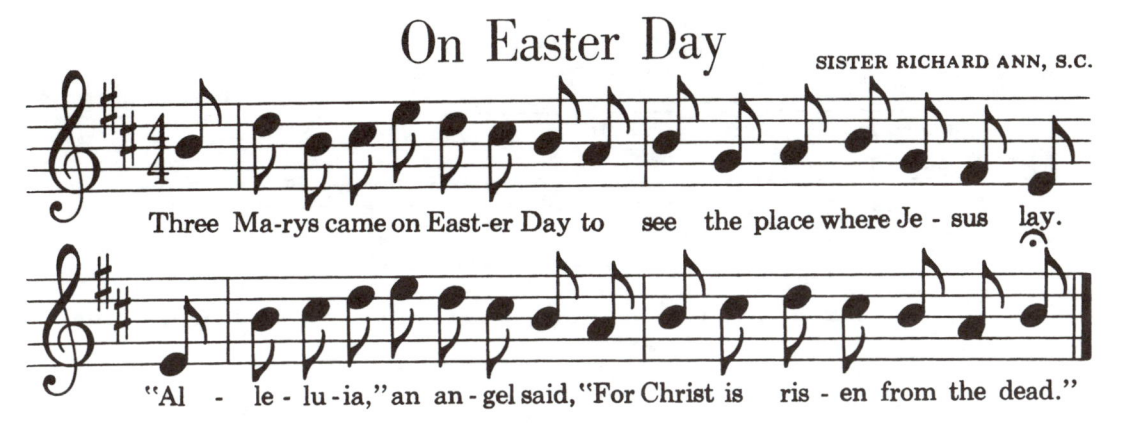

SISTER RICHARD ANN, S.C.

Three Marys came on Easter Day to see the place where Jesus lay.
"Alleluia," an angel said, "For Christ is risen from the dead."

The Annunciation

1. One day while Mary knelt in pray'r
   She saw an angel standing there.
   His glory filled the dwelling place,
   He said to her, "Hail, full of grace."

2. Now Mary feared and bowed her head.
   "Oh, do not fear," the angel said,
   "For God shall send His Son to thee.
   His holy Mother thou shalt be."

3. Then Mary spoke the blessèd word,
   "Behold the handmaid of the Lord,
   As thou hast said, so be it done."
   The Son of God became her Son.

Mary said: "Behold the handmaid of the Lord; be it done unto me according to thy word." *Luke 1:38*

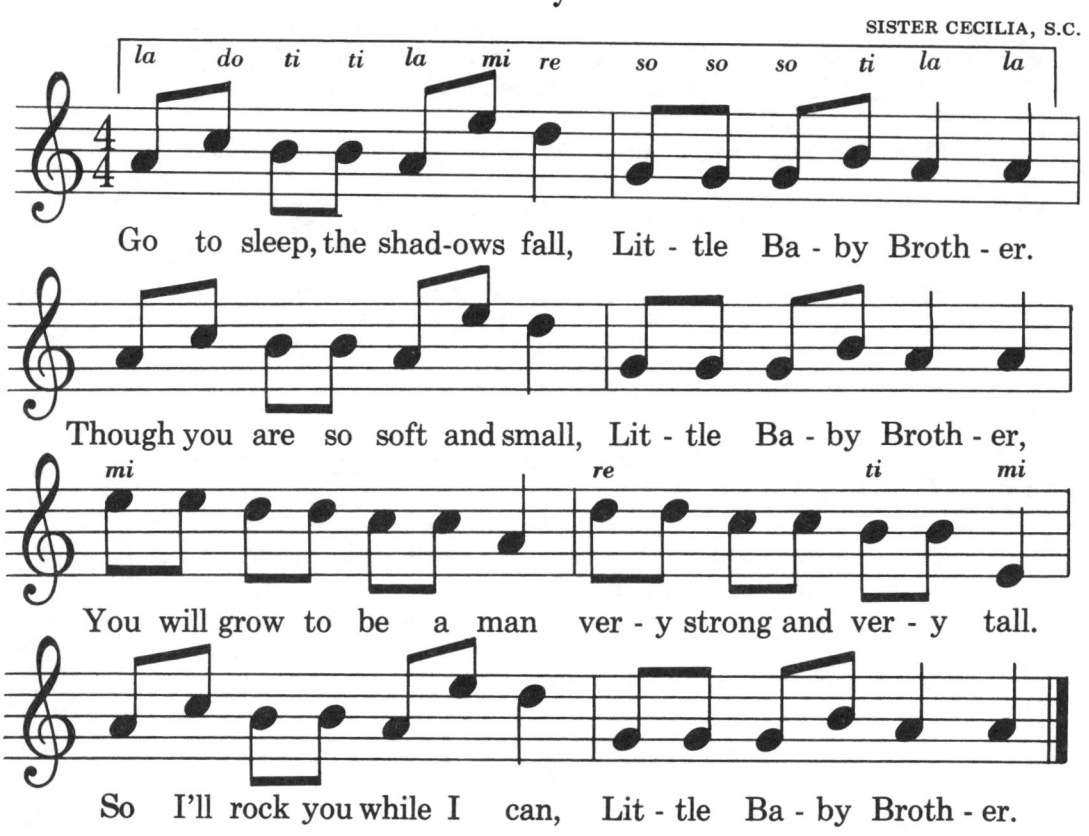

Little Baby Brother

SISTER CECILIA, S.C.

la do ti ti la mi re so so so ti la la

Go to sleep, the shad-ows fall, Lit-tle Ba-by Broth-er.

Though you are so soft and small, Lit-tle Ba-by Broth-er,

mi *re* *ti* *mi*

You will grow to be a man ver-y strong and ver-y tall.

So I'll rock you while I can, Lit-tle Ba-by Broth-er.

A Child's Good Night

OLD TUNE

1. Dear Lord, my eyes are full of sleep So long has been the day,
2. I know I need Thee al-ways near, So keep me in Thy sight

And I have giv-en up my toys For I am tired of play.
Un-til I come to Thee a-gain. Watch o'er me, Lord, this night.

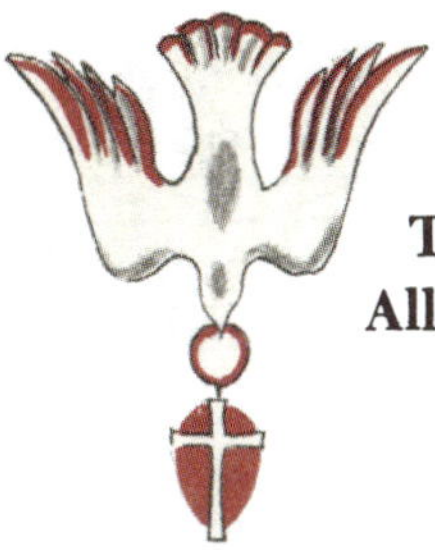

Pentecost

The Spirit of the Lord hath filled the whole world. Alleluia, alleluia.

Introit of Pentecost

Holy Spirit, Be My Light

DANISH

Ho - ly Spir-it, be my light Through the dark-ness of the night.
From Thy heav'n-ly throne a-bove, Oh, fill my heart with love.

To the Trinity

SISTER MARY ANTONE, C.S.J.

1. God the Fa-ther, God the Son, Ho - ly Spir - it, Three in One,
2. May we al-ways love Thy name, In our hearts Thy King-dom reign,
3. May we love Thee more and more, Serve Thee 'til our life is o'er,

Thee we praise and Thee a - dore.
May Thy will be done in us. A - men.
Ev - er Bless - ed Trin - i - ty.

My Little House

SISTER ANGELICA, S.C.

I have a lit-tle house and so do you, (and so do you)
I see the sun that's shin-ing ev-'ry-where, (oh, ev-'ry-where)

It's ver-y much a-live and yours is too, (and yours is too)
I hear the rob-in's song up-on the air, (up-on the air)

I count-ed all the doors and there were five, (and there were five)
I smell my moth-er's pies and taste them too, (and taste them too)

I count-ed all the doors, you count them too, (you count them too)
I touch our ba-by's hands so soft and new, (so soft and new)

One, two, three, four, five lit-tle doors!

What is the lit-tle house? (the lit-tle house)

If you can guess what the doors are, you will know what the house is.

Blessed Be God

SISTER ROSE MARGARET, C.S.J.

1. Bless - ed be God for the lit - tle birds,
2. Bless - ed be God for the pret - ty flow'rs,
3. Bless - ed be God for the sum - mer - time,

Bless - ed be God for the sky,
Bless - ed be God for the ground,
Bless - ed be God for the spring,

Bless - ed be God for the bil - low - y clouds
Bless - ed be God for the rain and the sun
Bless - ed be God for the beau - ti - ful world.

That swift - ly go sail - ing by.
And shad - y trees we have found.
To Him our praise we sing.

Chants to Our Lady

No. 1

1. Hear thy chil-dren, fair-est Moth-er: as our prayers to thee a - rise.
2. With our songs we come to praise thee, La-dy, Queen of Par - a - dise.

No 2.

1. Hail, sweet Virgin, pure and holy, thou our gentle Mother art.
2. Listen to thy children lowly; take us to thy loving heart.

Holy Mary, Blessed Mary

SISTER JOHN JOSEPH, C.S.J.

Holy Mary, Blessèd Mary, Mother of our Savior,

Holy Mary, Blessèd Mary, listen to our pray'r.

Purest lily, spotless virgin, Queen of all the angels,

Holy Virgin, Holy Mother listen to our pleading,

Listen to our pray'r.

WOLFGANG AMADEUS MOZART

Mozart was born more than two hundred years ago in Austria. His father was a musician in a court. When Wolfgang was only four years old he could pick out tunes on the piano. When his father heard him do this he started to give him music lessons.

At first Mozart used the music his father wrote for him. But after a short time he began to write some pieces for himself. He learned to play so well that his father took him and his sister to play for princes and other people in many big cities.

Wherever Mozart went people were made happy by his music. They gave him many gifts and honors. Even the Pope honored him.

You will like to sing his songs and play his pieces.

Dancing Long Ago

CARLA MARIA BIANCHI

WOLFGANG AMADEUS MOZART
From "THE MARRIAGE OF FIGARO"

Once long a-go while this mu-sic was play-ing
La-dies and gen-tle-men, grace-ful-ly sway-ing,
Danced to its rhy-thm so state-ly and slow,
Turn-ing and curt-sy-ing, bow-ing so low,—
Step-ping to mu-sic, state-ly and slow.

Minuet In F

WOLFGANG AMADEUS MOZART

Come, Dear Jesus

SISTER CECILIA, S.C.

Come, Dear Jesus, to my heart and stay with me for-ev-er.

I will be Your lov-ing child and You will leave me nev-er.

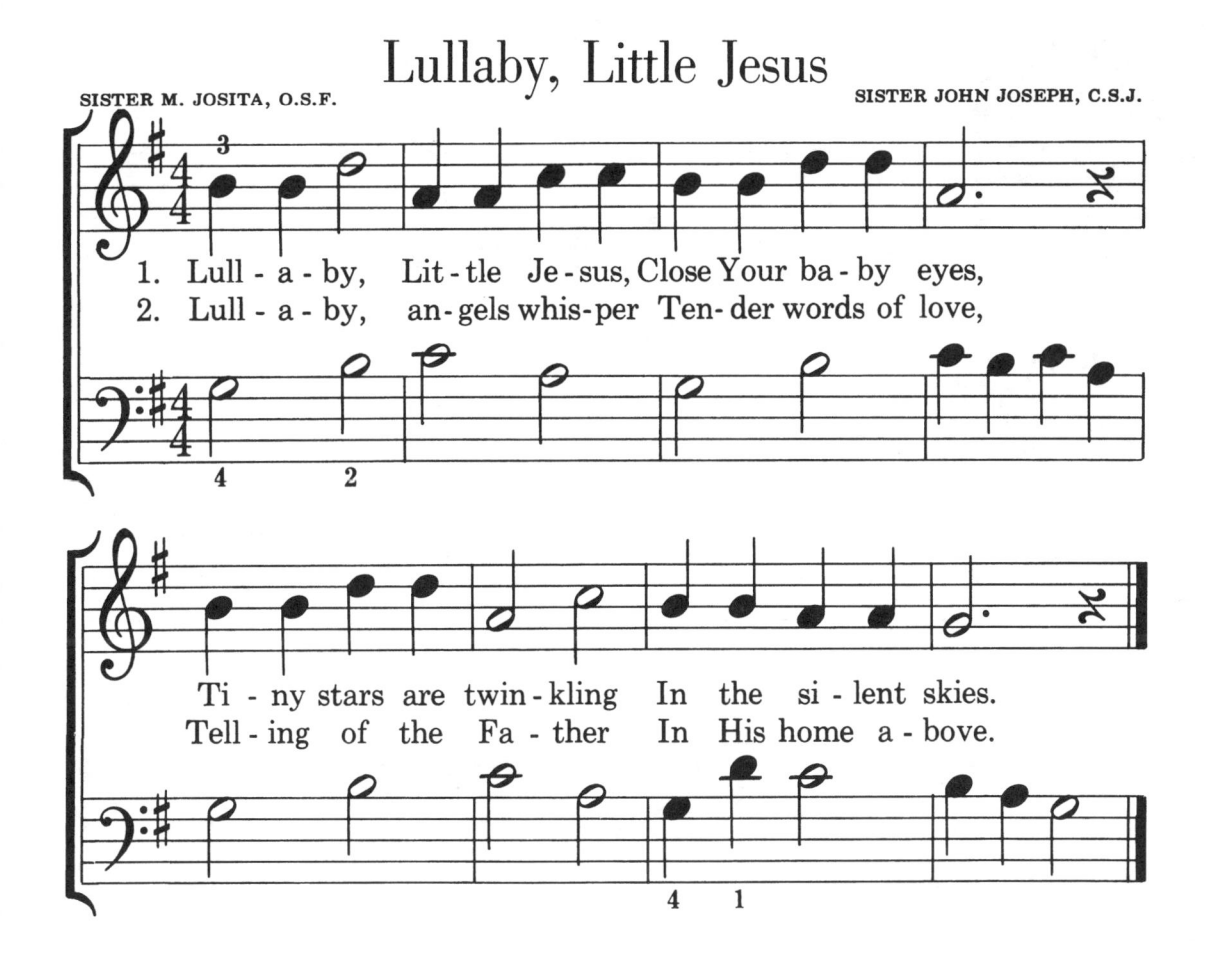

Lullaby, Little Jesus

SISTER M. JOSITA, O.S.F. SISTER JOHN JOSEPH, C.S.J.

1. Lull-a-by, Lit-tle Je-sus, Close Your ba-by eyes,
2. Lull-a-by, an-gels whis-per Ten-der words of love,

Ti-ny stars are twin-kling In the si-lent skies.
Tell-ing of the Fa-ther In His home a-bove.

Little Things

SISTER IMMACULATA, S.S.J. — S. R. M.

1. God loves the ver-y lit-tle things,
2. God loves the ti-ny flow-ers white,

The grass that grows in shad-y lane,
The but-ter-fly with yel-low wings,

The lit-tle lark that sweet-ly sings,
The lit-tle child who kneels at night

The lit-tle sil-ver drops of rain.
To pray to Him for lit-tle things.

Are the first and third phrases exactly alike?

Adiós, Reina del Cielo

MEXICAN

A-diós, Rei-na del Cie-lo, Ma-dre del Sal-va-dor.
O glo-rious Queen of Heav-en, O Moth-er of Our Lord.

A-diós, O Ma-dre mí-a, A-diós, a-diós, a-diós.
O glo-rious Queen of An-gels, You are my Moth-er too.

My Country

CAROL FULLER
AUSTRIAN MELODY

1. Man-y lands are fine; I love this land of mine;
2. Man-y lands are fine; I love this land of mine;

Moun-tains wear-ing robes of blue Seem to say, "I'm trust-ing you."
Sing-ing for-est, roll-ing sea Seem to say, "Be strong like me."

Man-y lands are fine; I love this land of mine.
Man-y lands are fine; I love this land of mine.

Saint Francis and the Wolf
By Sister Cecilia, S.C.

Once upon a time, in the little town of Gubbio, Italy, the people were very much worried. A big wolf lived in the forest near the town. Every day he came growling and growling out of the forest. He ran up and down the main street growling and growling. If he saw a goose or a duck he would eat it right up. He even ate up the sheep and cows and donkeys.

There was a wolf, a ver-y bad wolf,
a ver-y, ver-y, ver-y, ver-y, ver-y bad wolf,
And he ate up the cows, and he ate up the sheep,
and he ate up the chick-ens and the ducks and the geese,

And ev-'ry-bod-y knew that if he got a chance,

he'd eat up the peo-ple, too!

Everybody was afraid of the wolf. When they saw him coming they would all run into their houses and shut the doors tight.

(DRUM)
They shut all the doors with a bang!

(CYMBALS)
They shut all the win-dows with a bang!

(TAMBOURINE)
They shut all the shut-ters with a bang!

(ALL INSTRUMENTS)
Bang! Bang! Bang!

One day the mayor said, "We can't stay in the house all the time. We shall have to get rid of that wolf. Is anybody brave enough to go to the forest and capture the wolf?" But nobody was brave enough.

No - bod-y, no - bod-y, no - bod-y, no - bod-y,

Not a soul was brave e - nough

to go and catch the great big wolf.

No-bod-y, no-bod-y, no-bod-y, no-bod-y, no-bod-y!

The mayor was discouraged. The people were discouraged. They thought they would have to spend their whole lives running away from the wolf. Then a man said, "I know a man who is able to talk to the birds and fishes. Maybe he could talk to the wolf and ask him please to go away and live somewhere else."

The mayor said, "Tell him to come to Gubbio. We will give him lots of money to chase our wolf away."

But the man said, "He won't take any money. He doesn't care anything about money. His name is Francis. Some people say he is a saint."

Some people say that Francis is a saint,
Because his heart is filled with love,
With burning love for Christ Our Lord,
Because he loves all other men,
And even little birds and beasts,
Because he is so good and kind
To people who are poor and hungry,
Some people say that Francis is a saint.

So Francis came to Gubbio, and right away he went out to find the wolf. He sat down at the edge of the forest and waited. All the people locked themselves up in their houses and watched from the windows. Soon the big wolf came out of the forest.

The wolf came out of the for-est,
the wolf came out of the for-est,
The wolf came out of the for-est,
Oh! Oh! The peo-ple were a-fraid to look!

Francis stood up and went to meet the wolf. The wolf growled and was about to jump at him and eat him up. But Francis only smiled and held up his hand. The wolf was surprised that Francis was not afraid of him. He tilted his head on one side and looked at Francis. Francis began to talk softly to him, and the wolf began to listen.

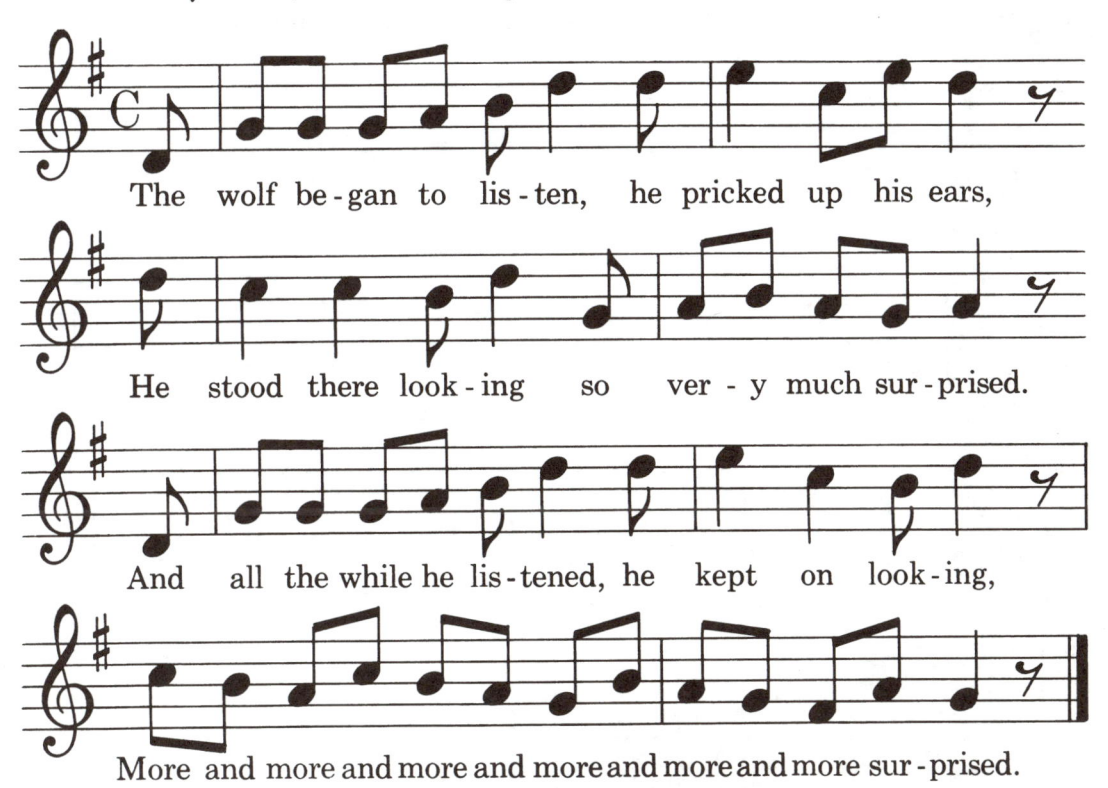

The wolf be-gan to lis-ten, he pricked up his ears,

He stood there look-ing so ver-y much sur-prised.

And all the while he lis-tened, he kept on look-ing,

More and more and more and more and more and more sur-prised.

Francis kept on talking softly to the wolf. Then the people saw the wolf sit down and cover his face with his big paws. "Well," they said, "just look at that." And Francis kept on talking to the wolf. This is what he said.

Aren't you a-shamed, Broth-er Wolf,
Aren't you a-shamed to be so bad?
All the chil-dren are a-fraid of you,
All the fa-thers and the moth-ers, too.
Oh, oh! Why are you so bad,
When you could be good in-stead?

Then Francis told the wolf about the good God who made all things and wanted all the people and all the animals to be happy in His beautiful world. He told the wolf that the good God wanted people and animals to be friends, and to be kind to each other. Oh, he told the wolf many things as they sat at the edge of the forest.

Soon the people who were looking out of their windows saw Francis patting the wolf on the head, and the wolf licking Francis' hands. Then they saw Francis hold out his hand to the wolf and the wolf put his big paw in it as a dog would do. "Well," said the people, "just look at that!"

Then Francis and the wolf started back to Gubbio together, singing as they went along:

Back to Gub-bi-o we go, Back to Gub-bi-o we go,
Back to Gub-bi-o we go, Fran-cis and his Broth-er Wolf.

Francis called all the people to come out of their houses. "I want you to meet Brother Wolf," he said. "He promises he will never frighten you again, or eat up your chickens or ducks or geese, if you will promise to feed him every day when he comes to town."

Well, of course, the people promised, and they kept their promise, too. And Brother Wolf was never bad again. He came to town every day for his dinner, and he was so kind that the little children could put their little arms around his neck, and even ride on his big shaggy back. This is the song they sang to him.

Broth-er Wolf, Broth-er Wolf, Please let me ride on your back to-day,

Up the street, down the street, Out to the for-est and back a-gain.

Do you know who Francis was? Well, he was really and truly a saint, and because he loved God so much, and loved all God's creatures so much, even the wolf of Gubbio would listen to him. Let's ask Saint Francis to help us love God, too, and always to be kind and good to everyone.

Saint Fran-cis help us all to be God's own lov-ing chil-dren,

Help us love our Fa-ther dear, Help us love each oth-er,

Help us to be kind and good, God's own lov-ing chil-dren.

We Sing the Mass

Kyrie Eleison

MASS XVIII

Ky - ri - e e - le - i - son. *iij.* Chri - ste — e - le - i - son. *iij.*
(*Lord, have mercy on us.*) (*Christ, have mercy on us.*)

Ky - ri - e e - le - i - son. *ij.* Ky - ri - e — e - le - i - son.
(*Lord, have mercy on us.*) (*Lord, have mercy on us.*)

When two notes are joined together in chant, sing the second note lighter and softer. In the last Kyrie hold the first of the three notes slightly longer.

After the Kyrie of the Mass the priest sings a prayer in Latin.

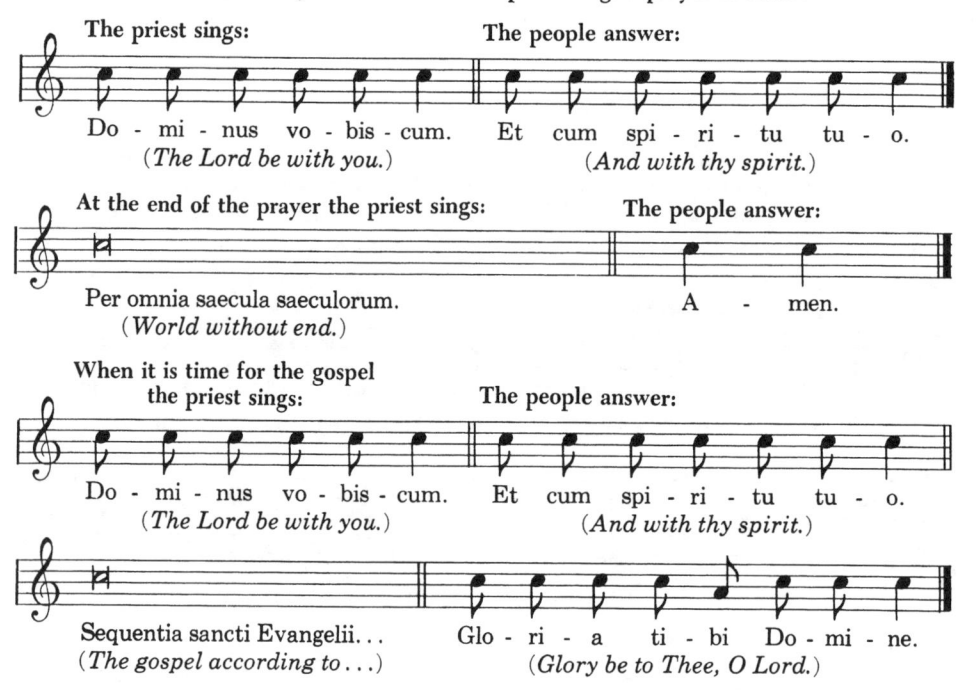

The priest sings: **The people answer:**

Do - mi - nus vo - bis - cum. Et cum spi - ri - tu tu - o.
(*The Lord be with you.*) (*And with thy spirit.*)

At the end of the prayer the priest sings: **The people answer:**

Per omnia saecula saeculorum. A - men.
(*World without end.*)

When it is time for the gospel the priest sings: **The people answer:**

Do - mi - nus vo - bis - cum. Et cum spi - ri - tu tu - o.
(*The Lord be with you.*) (*And with thy spirit.*)

Sequentia sancti Evangelii... Glo - ri - a ti - bi Do - mi - ne.
(*The gospel according to...*) (*Glory be to Thee, O Lord.*)

The Offertory

Before he begins the Offertory the priest sings: **The people answer:**

Do - mi - nus vo - bis - cum.   Et cum spi - ri - tu tu - o.
(The Lord be with you.)   *(And with thy spirit.)*

The Preface

Before he begins the most important part of the Mass the priest sings the Preface.

The priest sings: **The people answer:**

Per om - ni - a sae - cu - la sae - cu - lo - rum. A - men.
(World without end.)

Do - mi - nus vo - bis - cum.   Et cum spi - ri - tu tu - o.
(The Lord be with you.)   *(And with thy spirit.)*

Sur - sum cor - da.   Ha - be - mus ad Do - mi - num.
(Lift up your hearts.)   *(We do lift them to the Lord.)*

Gra - ti - as a - ga - mus Do - mi - no De - o nos - tro. Di - gnum et jus - tum est.
(Let us give thanks to the Lord, our God.)   *(It is fitting and just.)*

Sanctus

San - ctus, San - ctus, San - ctus Do - mi - nus De - us Sa - ba - oth. Ple - ni sunt cae -
(Holy, Holy, Holy, Lord God of Hosts.)

li et ter - ra glo - ri - a tu - a. Ho - san - na in ex - cel - sis.
(Heaven and earth are filled with Thy glory.)   *(Hosanna in the highest.)*

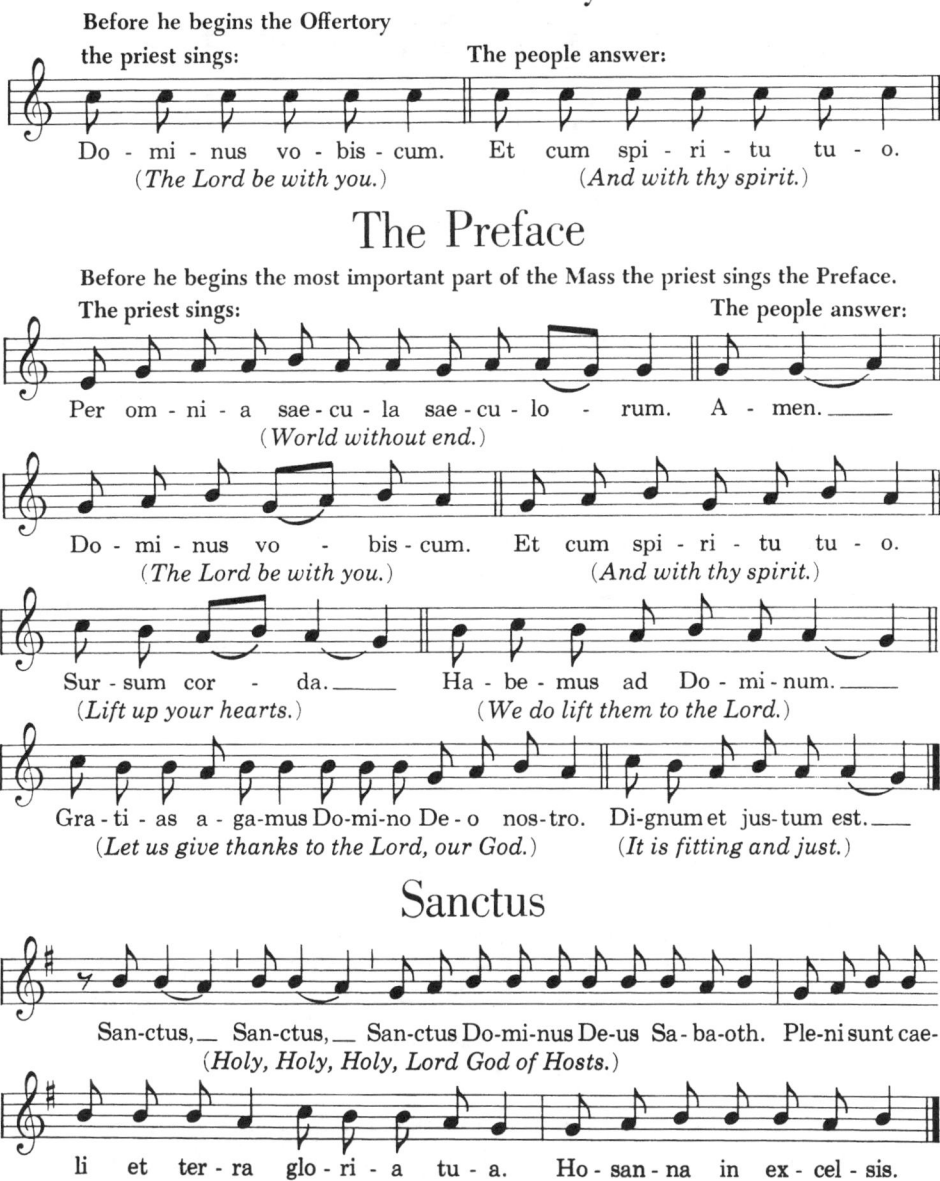

Sing the second syllable of the word "Sanctus" lightly and softly.

Benedictus

Be - ne - dic - tus qui ve - nit in no - mi - ne Do - mi - ni.
(Blessed is He Who comes in the name of the Lord.)

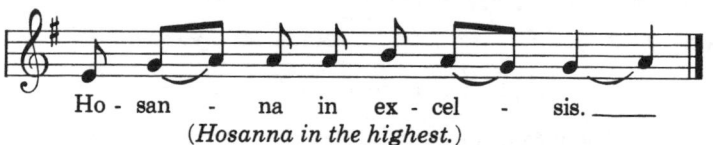

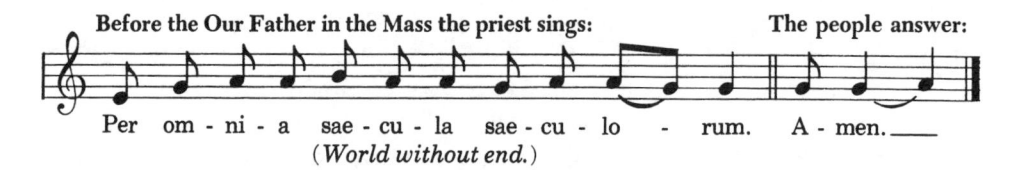

Ho - san - na in ex - cel - sis.
(Hosanna in the highest.)

Before the Our Father in the Mass the priest sings: **The people answer:**

Per om - ni - a sae - cu - la sae - cu - lo - rum. A - men.
(World without end.)

At the end of the Our Father the priest sings: **The people answer:**

Et ne nos in - du - cas in ten - ta - ti - o - nem. Sed li - be - ra nos a ma - lo.
(And lead us not into temptation.)   *(But deliver us from evil.)*

The Communion

A little while before the Communion of the Mass the priest sings: **The people answer:**

Per om - ni - a sae - cu - la sae - cu - lo - rum. A - men.
(World without end.)

Pax Do - mi - ni sit sem - per vo - bis - cum. Et cum spi - ri - tu tu - o.
(The peace of the Lord be always with you.)   *(And with thy spirit.)*

Agnus Dei

A-gnus De - i, qui tol-lis pec-ca-ta mun-di: mi-se-re-re no - bis.
(*Lamb of God, who takest away the sins of the world, have mercy on us.*)

A-gnus De - i, qui tol-lis pec-ca-ta mun-di: mi-se-re-re no - bis.
(*Lamb of God, who takest away the sins of the world, have mercy on us.*)

A-gnus De - i, qui tol-lis pec-ca-ta mun-di: do-na no-bis pa - cem.
(*Lamb of God, who takest away the sins of the world, grant us peace.*)

How should we sing the second note above "Dei"?

After the Communion of the Mass the priest sings another prayer in Latin.

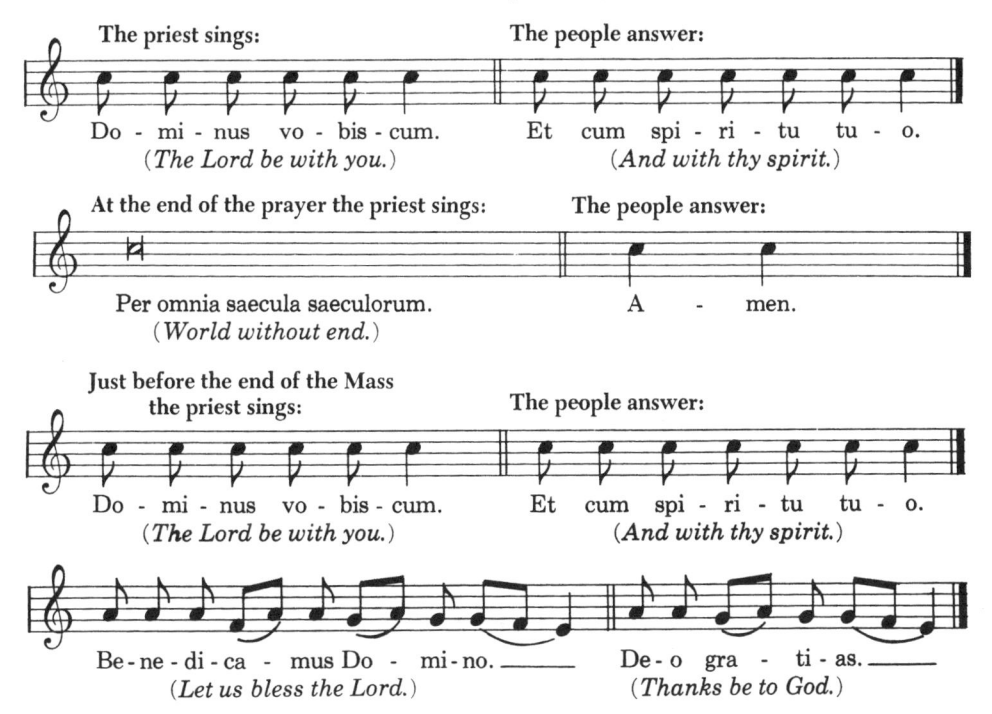

The priest sings:
Do - mi - nus vo - bis - cum.
(*The Lord be with you.*)

The people answer:
Et cum spi - ri - tu tu - o.
(*And with thy spirit.*)

At the end of the prayer the priest sings:
Per omnia saecula saeculorum.
(*World without end.*)

The people answer:
A - men.

Just before the end of the Mass the priest sings:
Do - mi - nus vo - bis - cum.
(*The Lord be with you.*)

The people answer:
Et cum spi - ri - tu tu - o.
(*And with thy spirit.*)

Be - ne - di - ca - mus Do - mi - no.
(*Let us bless the Lord.*)

De - o gra - ti - as.
(*Thanks be to God.*)